The One Entity

The Universe is Looking for New Innovators

Johnny Studstill Jr

Table of Contents

Chapter 1:

The Grand Launch

Anthony clicks send on another email. He knows Denise is going to roll her eyes tomorrow when she sees her inbox, but she'll handle it. The meetings have to get booked. Anthony doesn't care if he drops unconscious from exhaustion- he's going to speak to everyone. Apple. Microsoft. Even the Prime Minister of the goddamned United Kingdom. The word needs to get out. LevelUp is here, and it's going to change the world.

His phone buzzes in his pocket, but Anthony ignores it, mentally preparing himself for the week ahead. The texts he's receiving are all the same, anyway. There are hundreds of congratulation messages, but Anthony is sick of praise. Yes, he's pleased. Yes, he's excited. But the launch of the app is just the first step on a long journey. It isn't enough for Anthony. It'll only be enough when every man and woman in the world has access to LevelUp- the app that will make their business dreams come true.

A knock on the door makes Anthony look up, shocking him back to the present. He stands, then walks to the door to let Denise in. She's in a black dress- about the closest to party attire that Denise could handle. Even though she's about to go out and celebrate, Anthony knows she would sit down and plan a month's worth of scheduling if he asked her. She'd complain while she's doing it- she always gives him a hard time- but she'd get it done.

"You saw the emails?" Anthony says. "It's going to be a busy week, Denise, but we can't let this momentum die."

"There's a lot of people waiting for you, Tony."

"Tell them to go home. They all deserve a break."

"They did go home. Now they're back and apparently already running low on champagne."

Anthony glances at his watch- his father's, custom-built by an independent craftsman in Switzerland- and starts to laugh. Nine? He swears he was only sitting at his desk for an hour. He stands, turns off his monitor, and puts on his suit jacket. "I guess the time got away from me," he says. "Hard to stay in the present when the future is so exciting."

"Turn your brain off for a bit, Tony. You have to celebrate before the hard work starts."

"We'll have plenty more reasons to celebrate before long."

"And you'll have plenty more reasons to work. You've got a speech?"

Anthony taps the breast of his suit jacket. "I don't need one. It's going to come from here."

Denise sighs. "Nothing bothers you, does it? Sometimes, I think my job is just to be anxious on your behalf."

"Your job is to keep me sane," says Tony with a grin. He studies his reflection. It's a good job he got ready earlier. His Kiton suit still looks well pressed, sharp, just tight enough on his arms to show off his strength. His beard is short and trimmed to perfection- an arching neckline just beneath his chin, not a hair out of place. He sprays a dab of aftershave on his neck and wrists and rubs it in gently. Dior. Respectable, but muted.

"You've been in the office since seven in the morning, and you still manage to look like a guy from a catalog," says Denise. "How do you do it, Tony?"

"You've got to look the part to impress investors. I learned that the hard way." Another grin. "Let's go and meet them, shall we? They should be celebrating as well. Investing in NexCorp is probably about the most altruistic thing most of them have ever done."

***

Anthony sits in the passenger seat of his BMW as Denise drives the three minutes to the Generation Hotel. It was expensive to book out for a party, but Anthony wanted somewhere modern and- more importantly- somewhere close to the office. He can't be far from his desk, not when he has so much work to do.

The hotel is curved and elegant, jutting out away from the coast in an arch of mirrored walls that reflect the stars. It had only opened a month ago, and until now, Anthony had only seen it from a distance. It looks like a hotel from a science fiction film set in a Utopian era of the future.

"Have you been here yet?" Denise asks as she hands the car keys over to the valet waiting for them.

"Not yet," he says. "The parties I get invited to are at the Ritz. Most rich people in this city haunt the place like ghosts. Like they've forgotten there's other buildings outside."

"You wanted something a little more old-school?"

"The old school is done, Denise. This is perfect." Anthony breathes a sigh of satisfaction as he looks up at the hotel. He's going to enjoy today. That's not something he's normally very good at. He has a dogged attitude towards work, and he barely spends a moment thinking about anything other than his tasks for the next day. *Not today*, he tells himself. Today is about celebrating.

He looks at Denise and frowns. "Hey, what about this new guy you've been spending so much time with," he says. "I told you to invite him. Is he already here?"

Denise blushes for a moment. The woman was never very good at discussing her private life. "He's not really interested in this kind of thing," she says.

"Fair enough. As long as I get to meet him soon."

"You know I don't mix work and personal matters, Tony."

"Maybe break your rule, just for me, huh? I want to meet the guy who has managed to make you break your vow of single life forever."

Denise blushes again. Anthony grins. She's easy to tease. He tries not to do it too often, but it's still amusing to see the iron lady of business blushing like a schoolgirl.

The function room is just across from reception, through a glass corridor that lets the lights of the city shine through. He pushes through the door without a second thought and applause thunders in his ears.

"The man of the moment!"

"Well done, Mr. Brown."

"Bet you loved keeping us waiting!"

There are a hundred familiar faces there, all of them smiling, whooping, and shouting their praise. He smiles. Many of them are *his* people-people who trust him, who have never let him down before, even back in the old days when everyone called him a kook, a crackpot, a new-age socialist, a threat to society.

It was all nonsense. The crying death rattle of a bunch of CEOs and Tech Bros who have realized that their time was soon coming to an end. The future is going to be different. Anthony always believed it, but now, looking around at the fruits of his success, he knows it.

No expense has been spared on the party. The room is alive with color, cocktail dresses, and excitement. There's a pop-up bar in the corner handing out glasses of champagne, cocktails, bottles of beer- anything that anyone wants.

"Speech! Speech!" calls several people from inside the party. Anthony's only too happy to oblige them. He finds a spot right at the center of the room and taps the side of a glass with a spoon. Everyone falls quiet at once. There are dozens of eyes upon him. All wide. Expectant. He knows that they are all looking for encouragement. That they need to feel as though the momentum of their hard work is leading to something important. They're all aware of Anthony's important mission to change the landscape of business forever. But it's important to reinforce it for all of them as often as he can.

"When I was in business school, I realized that the world works best when businesses work as they were supposed to. Capitalism is meant to be about innovation through competition. Ideas turn to profit and wealth, and old successes are supposed to adapt to new challenges in order to stay relevant. The world is a series of organizations. Like cogs in a machine, they are all supposed to turn at the same time, propelling each other and keeping the world moving.

"But, for too long now, that hasn't been how the world has worked. Even here in Green City, the majority of wealth is held by companies that crush any competition that tries to come their way. They use their resources to stop smaller businesses from operating successfully before they even have a chance to test their fresh new ideas. That means no new jobs are created. No wealth is moved around the city. This means that the gap between the rich and poor has been growing. To the point where rich people can't begin to imagine how the poorest live, and the poorest can't begin to believe the extravagance that the rich exhibit. People in the poorest parts of the world might have the best business ideas ever, but how are they supposed to start? They can't afford the exorbitant rents that the rich charge for their offices. They don't have access to investors. They don't have the money they need to get started.

"LevelUp is the link in the chain that they need. Together, we have created a platform where the richest in society come together with anyone who needs help to fund their ideas and get them started. Our hard work has made all of this possible. When I started NexCorp, I was just a kid with a dream. I didn't have the knowledge and experience, nor the manpower, that I needed to turn my dream into a platform that works."

"This party isn't for me," he says- loud enough for people to hear but still in the same calm and collected tone he always uses. The crowd holds their breath. "It's for all of you. For making my dream a reality. NexCorp is going to become the face of a new generation of business. And I mean business as it was meant to be a way for *all* people to get a shot at wealth. We're at the brink of a new world, people. A world where no good idea gets shot down or is dead in the water for lack of funds." He grins. "This is where the fun begins."

Anthony tries to meet the eye of every person who helped him get to this point. Moira Bentley, his head of business strategy, spent the last eight weeks working long into the night, even when he told her not to. Bruce Bright, his tech whiz and head of IT security, spent hours and hours of meetings patiently tuning and tweaking the LevelUp app until it matched the vision in Anthony's dreams.

And, of course, Denise. She steps backward into the crowd, joining the rest of the well-wishers. No one there knows her like Anthony does. She's been there through the hardest of times, soothing him as they went from boardroom to boardroom when investors were slamming doors in his face. To the rest of the office, she's just a PA: someone with responsibilities but without any real power. To Anthony, she's his lifeline. He can't imagine what he would have done without her. He tries to flash her a smile- to meet her eyes so that she can see how much she means to him, but for some reason, she's looking at her feet. *Probably uncomfortable*, Anthony thinks. She never was all that good with being in the limelight. But that's what makes her a great PA. She never puts herself first.

There are other people in the party as well- many of whom Anthony does not recognize and who most likely consider him to be the devil. They're there to keep an eye on what his app is all about and how much of a threat it poses to their vested interests. *Well, let's tell them what they need to hear*, Anthony thinks.

"LevelUp is the next trend in global business. The most important development since the industrial revolution." He holds up his smartphone. "All anyone needs to use it is one of these. Anyone can post a business plan on LevelUp, and it will be seen by thousands of the world's most savvy, wealthy investors. Anyone can get connected to money. Their ideas will come to life. Only those projects that have the maximum benefit for society will find their way to the top of the news feeds. This is what business needs. Governments won't help. Most people out there don't want to share what they've got. But sharing is what people need if they're going to create their own wealth. The ladder is back in business, and now anyone can start climbing."

Whoops. Cheers. Tears. Anthony can tell at a glance who his people are and who they are not. His people believe in him. They work for him because they know that NexCorp can change the world.

***

As Anthony wraps up his speech, some launch party guests begin to gather at the fringes of the room, away from the lights and the swirls of laughter. They clap politely, but they have hard eyes. They sip their champagne with reservation, as though it's leaving a bad taste in their mouth. Anthony can't help but grin. He expected his launch party to get infiltrated. There's a good reason he made it an open event, sending out invites to just about anyone he could think of. They need to see. They need to know that their time is coming.

As he's scanning the room, he pauses. One man isn't smiling or even pretending to clap. He sits hunched in a chair, his arm around the top of the backrest. His heavy frame fills the chair and some of the space around it besides. In the dim fringes of the room, Anthony can only make out half of his face, but that's enough for Anthony to recognize him. Robert Chambers of Chambers Energy. Anthony suppresses a shiver that tries to run up his spine. He didn't think the man would come in person. Chambers never turned up anywhere without a good reason- not when he could send his corporate cronies in his stead.

Anthony can't help but feel as though Chambers had been a specter hanging over him the whole of his life. As a kid, he spent far more time than he would have liked in Chambers's company. Their families were close friends and went on skiing trips together to the Alps. Though Anthony was a kid back then, he still remembered Chambers as an entitled, dominating teenager, a bully who wasn't afraid to make unreasonable demands. Later, when Anthony attended the Green City Institute for Enterprise, he couldn't avoid the Chambers leering presence. The man was a major shareholder in the business school and stopped Anthony whenever he could to dress him down and mock him for his ideas. From his tutors, Anthony had heard rumors of what Chambers had been like when he was a student at the school himself. He charmed girls from every dorm room when he first met them, but they'd end up hating him a few months later. It didn't matter to Chambers. So long as he got what he wanted from people.

Now, Anthony wants to talk to the man who overhung his life, but he can't take three steps through the function room without someone else from his company coming to speak to him. He tries his best to keep a smile on his face, but it quickly starts to get annoying.

"Enough with the congratulations!" he says. "I've got people to speak to."

Moira catches his eye with a smirk. "Working even now, aren't you, Mr. Brown?"

"I'll explain later, Moira." Then, in a lower whisper, he adds. "Get these people away from me."

Ever loyal and unwavering, Moira catches the urgency in his voice. She turns to the group of well-wishers and distracts them with one of her many tales of her exotic past traveling the world. *She's the opposite of Denise*, Anthony thought. *Confident and outgoing. A woman of the world.*

He peers over the top of the heads of the crowd of people and sees that Chambers is no longer sitting in his chair. He's stood, holding a cigar between two fingers, putting on a coat in readiness to leave.

Oh no, you don't, thinks Anthony, as he pushes his way through the crowd, ignoring the pleas for attention from his loyal staff. He marches straight over to Chambers and catches him just before he can leave the launch party.

"Robert," he says. "Leaving so soon?"

"Just keeping an eye in on our up-and-coming star," says Robert. Is voice rough and gravelly, coarse from years spent smoking those expensive Cubans? "I've seen enough, Little Tony. I think you're losing your mind."

Little Tony. That was his nickname for Anthony when they were kids. Chambers had been a teenager when Anthony was just starting school. Now, Anthony towered over the man. When he looked down, he could see the salt and pepper flecks surrounding the bald spot right at the top of Chambers's cranium.

"I think you're losing your cool," said Anthony. "People like you can't hold onto what you have forever; surely you know that."

"You're still repeating that crackpot philosophy your professors drummed into you then? What was it? *The world is a series of organizations helping each other."* He says this last sentence in a childish, mocking tone. "Tosh, lad. The world is made up of people: people who give and people who take. The givers lose. That's why this plan of yours won't work." Chambers asks him to leave again, but Anthony puts an arm between him and the door. He has no intention of letting the Chambers have the last word. Chambers sighed. "What do you want, Little Tony?" he says.

"I want to know why you're here personally. It can't be for any good reason."

"Because your business model threatens everything I stand for. So I needed to see for myself what you have to say about it." He grins, putting the cigar between his teeth. "What I've heard hasn't worried me, so you haven't got to worry either. I wish you all the luck in the world, lad."

Anthony goes to argue, but his phone buzzes in his pocket yet again. This time, it doesn't stop- a series of vibrations, one after another, demanding his attention. He steps aside, and Robert Chambers passes him by, his body just inches from Anthony's. The reek of stale smoke and alcohol on the older man's breath was enough to make Anthony gag. As Chambers leaves, Anthony is irritated that the situation between them is still unresolved. Chambers had been accused of business sabotage and intellectual property theft before. He'd never been charged with anything, but Anthony knew what the man was capable of.

Anthony looks at the phone that's been so violently buzzing in his pocket. As he looks, he exhales slowly, bringing a finger up and resting it over his lips. It isn't what he was expecting. It's a series of text messages from an unknown number, all saying the same thing over and over again.

"Beware, Anthony. Game time has begun."

Where other men would feel panic, Anthony feels a sharp focus. He scans the room with his searching green eyes, trying to see if there is anyone else there who looks suspicious. This was the second odd thing to happen during his launch party. Could the two be linked? He had been speaking to Chambers when the messages started sending. He supposes anyone could have been sending the messages on the Chambers's behalf. Equally, he knows how many enemies he already has in the corporate world of Green City. And, by launching his app that day, he has most likely picked up a few more in the last 24 hours.

The phone buzzes again. Anthony looks down. Two more messages- both hyperlinks to news articles. The first takes him to an interview he recently carried out with Forbes, where he described his plan to balance the economic system. The second takes him to a business report he had completed and sent to publishing just a week before so that it could be placed on the company website. The report outlines their business strategies for how they can continue to make LevelUp free for consumers.

So whoever it is isn't happy with what I'm doing, he thought. *Hardly narrows it down.*

He realizes that he's not going to get any more clues tonight. He also doesn't want to trouble anyone else- not even his closest allies- with what he's been sent. This is their night to celebrate their launch.

Anthony fades back into the party, playing the part of excited, energized CEO. He doesn't have to pretend too hard. As concerned as he is, he knows he is in control of the situation. He has always known he was going to make enemies. To him, this texting nonsense and Chambers's shoving his sweaty face in his business are all just signs that he's doing the right thing. Getting in the right people's faces. Making changes that hurt those who don't like to be hurt.

Chapter 2:

Unveiling Threats

"Can you get some coffee in here?" Anthony whispers to Denise as his core team comes into the boardroom.

They look worse for wear. Pale, some of them rubbing their temples with the tips of their fingers. They'd partied hard the night before, just like Anthony wanted them to do. He supposes he forgot about hangovers. He doesn't get hangovers, but they seem like too much of a waste of time.

"Look alive, people," he says aloud, turning on the interactive screen behind him. "We have big things to discuss."

"It couldn't wait until after lunch?" says Bruce Langlow. He's head of I.T. security and always has to be the smartest person in the room, even when he isn't. If it weren't for him being so damned reliable and efficient, Anthony guesses he would have fallen out with the guy a long time ago. "You know that this really isn't an efficient way of working, Mr. Brown. In fact, studies show that most employees are able to better complete tasks and make decisions when they have fresh glucose in their system, injected in the form of food."

"I expect my core team to be able to work their way through a headache," he says. "Some problems can't wait. This is important, guys, so I need you to tell me that you're with me, focused, and ready to act."

The serious tone in his voice causes them to perk up. Moira frowns, leaning forward with her brows furled. Ken opens his notebook- he looks palest out of all of them, but he's still ready to work. Bruce doesn't change his expression at all; he just sits up straighter in his seat. The other key representatives from H.R., marketing, and sales all fall silent. They know when to listen and when to argue. Anthony always provides his team the freedom to voice their opinions, and he isn't afraid of criticism. But he also makes sure that his team knows the difference between play time and work time. Anthony is many things- but he isn't a time waster. Work is work for a reason, and they have big problems to solve.

With a few taps on his phone screen, Anthony projects it onto the larger wall behind them. He puts the text messages from last night in front and center. His core team reads the messages with widening eyes.

"I began receiving this at about quarter past nine last night," he says. "Just when I was talking to Robert Chambers."

"God," says Bruce. "I know you, Anthony. You didn't threaten him, did you?"

"We were just catching up. But that isn't important."

"This is a security matter, you know. You should really have come to me first, Anthony, rather than calling this board room here!"

Anthony flashes him a warning look with his eyes. Bruce realizes he's crossed the mark- everyone around the boardroom is glaring at him as well. He backs down, looking at the desk and apologizing.

"I didn't want to ruin the festivities last night," says Anthony. "This didn't seem worth ruining anything else. They're just text messages- but I just wanted to make everyone aware of them, in case anyone else gets something similar."

Bruce opens his mouth to speak again, then stops himself. He doesn't interrupt this time- he's learned his lesson- but he still looks anxious.

"What's the matter, Bruce?" Anthony says again.

"These aren't just text messages, boss. That second link goes to the report you filled out yourself."

"I know. I sent it to get put on the website last week."

"But it never got put on the website. I stopped it from becoming public- there were too many business strategies on there. I wanted to review it and censor it a bit before it was available to be accessed."

"You never told me about this."

"I made a security judgment."

"NexCorp is for the people. They should know exactly what we're doing."

"This isn't an argument for here," Moira interjects. "The point is, whoever sent these messages somehow has access to internal documents that they shouldn't be able to see. That's much more of a problem, Anthony. So let's discuss this together."

Anthony is too calm and collected to blush, but he still feels a flash of embarrassment. He let Bruce get under his skin too often. *There is a reason you keep the man around*, he reminds himself. Bruce knows his job, and he knows security. He wouldn't have prevented the document from getting published without a good reason.

Thankfully, the tension gets defused as Denise returns. She has two large pots of coffee with her. Everyone pours themselves a cup except for Anthony. He hasn't drunk coffee for years. He likes to keep his wits sharp, unaffected by any sort of drug or stimulant, even one as benign as caffeine. He doesn't think coffee does anything that a gym session couldn't do anyway. After thirty minutes of rowing machine each morning, he feels as awake and alert as he needs to be to do his job well.

"We need to be vigilant," he says to his board room. "I trust every single person here. For now, I'm not even sure how much we have to worry. But it's time for us to keep our eyes ahead and alert. This launch is only just starting, and we can't let anything stop LevelUp from reaching the people who need it."

"I'll see what I can find out," says Bruce. "Maybe we've been hacked. I'll look into the security information as soon as this meeting's done."

Anthony nods. "Thank you, Bruce." He isn't going to let his pride or a petty squabble stop him from thanking Bruce. The man is an I.T. expert. If there's any issue with security, then he's going to find it. He finds himself relaxing. *They're just texts.* He supposes that he's been so worried about this launch for such a long time that anything unexpected is going to get magnified.

"Great. Time for the important stuff then." He grins. "We've got the most single-day downloads of any app in history- seven hundred thousand in twenty-four hours. How are we going to keep that pace going, Moira."

Moira is already on her feet, handing out copies of her business strategy plan to every person in the room. Of course, she's already five steps ahead. As Anthony watches his team talk, he feels pride. Even with their bellies filled with last night's champagne, they're still just about the best business team that he could ever have hoped for.

***

Anthony's afternoon is a whirlwind. He signs on three new investors in just a few short hours, whizzing from one part of the green city to the next. He speaks to representatives from IBM, Goldman Sachs, and even investors from the worlds of fashion, food, and infrastructure. "That's the beauty of LevelUp," he tells them. "This is an app without limits. A place for any and all different investors in any industry at all. You see a list of good ideas in front of them, and you choose the ideas you want to turn into a reality."

Most of them are people who, just a few months before, wouldn't even agree to a meeting. Now, they took his hand with pleasure, patting him on the back and congratulating them. Other people might feel spiteful at how two-faced it all was, but Anthony knows how business works. They're treating him seriously because they know this is serious. They know that LevelUp is going to change the world, and they're trying to get ahead of the curve.

But it's the last meeting of the day that he's looking forward to the most. He knows what his biggest investment opportunities are- Walker Solutions, Z Inc., and Phillip Sterling. Along with Chambers Energy, those companies were known as the "Big Four," the four most profitable companies in the entire city.

Opposite him, in his own boardroom, is Kelly Walker. She is CEO of Walker Solutions, a green energy company that has already secured hundreds of contracts to revolutionize the power grid in the state. She's an old-school hippy woman turned corporate leader.

Next to her is Rick Yewtree of Phillip Sterling. He barely manages a smile when Anthony nods at him. Yewtree has been very resistant to investing, but Anthony is hoping to make the cold man change his final.

Finally, there is Helda Zenata of Z Inc- an A.I. Tycoon who has just as ambitious plans for the future as Anthony. Her fortune had almost doubled in the last five months with the successful launch of her chatbot software.

Three investors. Three huge personalities. But between them, they have enough money to take LevelUp into the stratosphere.

Anthony goes into the boardroom with maximum energy, ready to put on a face for sales to wow these big three investors. He is buoyed completely from a day of success, filled with a sense of momentum that shows no sign of slowing down.

He tells them everything. How he sees the world as a series of organizations, all of whom are strongest and survive for longer when they support each other. He reminds them how many poor people there are in Green City and beyond who will never get to see their dreams of wealth and good ideas come to life. He reminds them of the inevitability of change- telling them who he has managed to get on his side already. He provides a series of what he considers to be impressive names and begins to wrap up his presentation.

"And that's the idea, ladies and gentlemen," Anthony says, flashing a grin at the three faces opposite. "By funding us now, you'll be accelerating the speed of our product launch. We can get started straight away, and tomorrow, your money will start finding its way into people's pockets, ready to help all of them."

He pauses, still grinning, expecting an applause.

The faces opposite him are quite stoic. Sterling, in particular, has his nose upturned as though he has just encountered a bad smell. "So you've come in here to tell us that you want to challenge our business model by presenting potential competitors with limitless funds? You're essentially telling us that you're planning for our downfall if I've heard you correctly?"

Anthony is taken aback. He blinks a couple of times before answering. "I'm talking about new opportunities- a chance for you all to spread some of your wealth around. You help a new business grow, and maybe they can support you in the future. Plus, you'll get a small share of their business that will earn you money."

"How small?"

"We allow for a five percent share of business purchased through the system- at maximum. That's to protect our new business startups. We want to give them the best chance for survival."

At that, Walker starts to laugh. She has a great laugh- all deep and soulful, and he pats Sterling on the back as she does so. "I think what Mr. Brown is telling us, Sterling, is that we had better sign up or get ready to be signed against, don't you? I have to admire your brashness, Mr. Brown." She closes her notebook and reaches out a hand. "I have to admit, I think it's a great idea. You have my support all the way. You can announce our involvement."

Once Mrs. Walker agrees, the other business leaders there sign on as well. Anthony can't quite believe his luck. In one day, he's managed to make an additional 25% of all the money hosted on the platform so far.

He's never going to get Chambers, but three out of the four largest businesses is still more than enough to get started. "My own "Big Three," he tells them. "Great to be doing business with you."

***

It's seven in the evening when Anthony finally gets back to the office. There are a few stragglers, but it's mostly quiet. Anthony walks through, giving smiles and waves, but his smile vanishes when he gets to his own office room. He sits at his desk and opens his calendar at once, scanning over the investors he has to speak to the next day. They're all important people from the entertainment world. He's already printed off several user profiles with new ideas for the entertainment industry that he intends to pitch to them.

It was all coming together. Regular people were getting their ideas into Anthony's briefcase, and he was making sure that big-wigs took them seriously. He knows he won't have to keep going around places face to face forever. Eventually, enough investors will be on board with the platform, and they'll be looking out for business ideas themselves. The platform will become a social network for moving money, and it'll get bigger than any single investor in the world.

That's his vision. Ever since he was at business school, he has always looked at the bigger picture behind every single lecture he had on marketing, strategy, and economics. It was obvious to him that the world is not made up of companies, all with their own interests. The world is a series of networks- all supporting and benefiting from one another. Of course, there is competition- competition is healthy and leads to innovation. However, competitors only get so far by building on the ideas of the person before. Everyone is linked. Everyone's fortunes affect the fortunes of others. Or they can, as long as the money reaches the right people.

Anthony carries out his prep for the next day and notices with satisfaction that he hasn't once thought of the strange texts that day. That's good- he doesn't need himself to be distracted. It shows that his mindfulness meditations and mindful exercise routines that he carries out each day are working to his benefit. He is keeping his mind clear and focused on what he wants to achieve.

***

"You're not planning to sleep here, are you?"

Anthony looks up. Denise is at the doorway again, already wearing a coat. If she had a coat on, then it had to be late. Denise was always first to the office and last to leave.

"Nine again?"

"Try nine forty-five. I hope you haven't been letting all of those news stories get in your head."

"I've just been prepping for meetings tomorrow." He frowns. "What news stories?"

"You really don't look at anything except for work! Didn't you wonder why everyone has been looking so anxious today?"

"I just guess everyone's busy. I never get time to look at the news."

Denise rolls her eyes and then pulls her phone out of her pocket. She holds it in front of Anthony's face, and Anthony squints to figure out what's going on in the video. When he sees a face, he recognizes it all too well; he can't help but scowl.

Chambers and a bunch of other old-money business types had an audience of congressmen, tech leaders, and other influential people. It looks like someone threw together something in response to LevelUp's launch. There was a big sign behind the Chambers on the wall- a banner that read "The Balance Conference." It's embossed with a familiar logo- A capital C and a capital E- in big blue letters underlined: Chambers Energy.

"The facts are that there has been a rise in investments that are unregulated, not properly assessed, and they are coming from people with no knowledge of markets," Chambers says in the video. "The sad part is that these great, rich, successful people are throwing away their money on things that won't work- that won't ever work. There's a reason that the big names are big names. They are the best, most successful business models. We can't pretend that random people across the world know better than they do!"

"He sounds desperate," says Anthony. "I'm not worried."

"Look at the audience, Tony. People are *clapping*. Some of those people have a lot of sway. What if he makes people afraid of us."

"They won't be afraid anymore when they can see what LevelUp can do."

"Your staff are getting worried. We should spend some time on countering this."

"Then get someone on it. I'm busy this week."

"This is more important than investors."

"Nothing is more important than investors right now, Denise. You just worry about getting me more meetings. I'll worry about Chambers."

Denise's mouth becomes a hard line. She nods and straightens her back. Anthony knows that she must be really upset. He knows Denise well, and knows that the only time she can't relax around him is when she's pissed off. She leaves, and Anthony watches through the window as she gets in her car and drives away. It's just him in the office now. He sighs.

He shouldn't raise his voice at her or anyone; he knows that. But he's been planning the launch of his product for years, and he knows he's going to have to stay single-minded if he's going to succeed. Investors were the key- they had to be the key. If LevelUp didn't have real money for it, then who would use it?

But perhaps Denise *does* have a point. Those people were listening to Chambers. Clapping their hands and nodding because Chambers has that way with people. LevelUp is there to help people, and Chambers Energy just wants to take their money and pollute their rivers. But that doesn't matter if Chambers can convince everyone that NexCorp is the *real* threat. It's classic scapegoat tactics. Stuff that isn't to do with business or community investment. Which means it isn't really his wheelhouse.

He tries to call Denise, but she doesn't pick up. He sends her a text instead, apologizing and asking her if she can work with Moira to plan a strategy to counter Chambers and his stupid Balance Conference. *I'll start tomorrow*, she replies five minutes later.

Anthony gives a sigh of relief. He needs Denise on his side; he knows that. Denise is an excellent P.A. and an open-hearted woman. But, for all her anxieties and her lack of confidence in herself, the woman knows how to hold a grudge with passion.

He stands up to go, then finds himself sitting down again and turning on his monitor. He can't help it- Anthony finds himself watching the video of Chambers again. *What is it about this guy?* Anthony wonders. He doesn't ever seem to be able to let things go. He's always had his eye on Anthony, dogging his career. No matter what ideas Anthony came up with, Chambers seemed to have an eye over it somehow, criticizing it. What is it about this guy that makes him so obsessed?

Anthony guesses that, in many ways, Chambers is more like him than anyone else he knows. The man knows what he wants and doesn't stop until he has it. He's made an enemy of Anthony, and he isn't going to stop trying to blow holes in his credibility.

Well, thought Anthony. *Perhaps it's time I started fighting fire with fire, my old friend.*

***

The next morning, Anthony receives a text that makes his heart sink.

I'm feeling under the weather today. I'm going to need to take a rest day. Sorry. Denise.

It's the first day off that his Personal Assistant has taken in all the time she's worked under him. It fills Anthony with a sense of dread- now is definitely not the time. He hates to admit that he needs the help, but he does. He has dozens of interviews lined up, and he has no idea how he's going to manage his time. Especially not now, with Chambers and his meddling fresh in his mind.

Anthony pumps the frustration out on his treadmill and then his exercise bike. He runs for ten kilometers that morning and cycles for twenty. It takes time, but Anthony needs to burn off anxious energy so he can stay focused. He grits his teeth as the sweat pours off his back. Exercise doesn't come easy today. It's like he's running uphill. *A bit like this product launch*, he thinks to himself warily. The grapefruit he eats for breakfast is bitter. The drive to the office is marked by congestion.

He arrives at the office twenty minutes later than he expected, and he's angry about it. His life is structured; it follows a routine. And it's not like he can get started straight away. Normally, Denise will start the day by providing him with his agenda of meetings and tasks. Now he has to sit and create it himself, his brow furled as he clicks on the keyboard of his computer.

It's nearly impossible. No combination of scheduling seems to give him enough time to travel the city and get from one location to the next. He has no idea how long Ubers take to get from place to place these days. Those finer details are for Denise to worry about.

Things feel out of control. He knows he was the one who upset Denise, but he can't shake the feeling that it's somehow all Chambers's fault. All of this was supposed to be going smoothly. LevelUp is supposed to be the start of the future, not a drain on his energy and time. He's never felt outmatched before, but now he feels as though Chambers is one step ahead.

Anthony can't help himself. He carried out an internet search for Chambers's "Balance Conference" and found himself reading the associated news stories.

"New App threatens to imbalance the world economy," says Forbes.

"Interview with Robert Chambers," says The Economist. "The man warning of a new wave of socialism in America."

"Who is Anthony Brown? A biography of the new "tech bro" who wants to take your money," says Fox News.

All of it leaves a bitter taste in his mouth. He has always been expecting a backlash and for many people not to agree with him. But it feels as though Chambers has managed to start a campaign to undermine him quicker than he could have prepared for it. Almost as though he has been preparing the media for a long time in advance. But that can't be possible, can it? He has made sure that they've kept everything about LevelUp completely secret.

In anger, Brown clears his morning schedule. He takes out his phone and calls Moira.

"I'm clearing my morning," he says. "I need you in my office."

"You've been reading the news then, sir?"

"Get Bruce. Don't tell anyone else. I just need people I can trust on this."

Moira takes a sharp intake of breath. Probably, she can hear the urgency in his voice. Anthony isn't one to usually lose his cool under normal circumstances.

***

They arrive in a matter of minutes. Moira looks worried, her blue eyes open wide and her fingers twitching nervously. Bruce looks harassed, as if he wasn't planning to start work yet. His tie is loose around his neck, and he smells like his first-morning cigarette.

"We're wall to wall at the moment, Anthony," he says. "We need some warning if you're going to call a meeting."

"Just listen for once, Bruce," says Moira.

Bruce raises an eyebrow at her. "I didn't realize you had been promoted to head of I.T. Moira, ordering me like that."

"I'm ordering you to listen," says Anthony. "This is not a normal meeting."

That makes him focus. He sits up in his chair and starts wearing a worried face that matches Moira's. Bruce was an argumentative guy; there was no question about it, but he ultimately knew which way his bread was buttered. Anthony was not usually a hard taskmaster, but he couldn't keep the edge out of his voice anymore.

"Something isn't right about all of this noise from Chambers. It's like he's setting a plan in motion, coordinating a concentrated media attack on Nexcorp and on LevelUp," he says. "He must be behind the document leak. He must have some way of accessing information in the company."

"Corporate espionage?" says Bruce.

"We're being hacked. I'm sure of it."

"That's not possible. You asked me to make security watertight, Anthony. That's what I've done."

"Somethings not right. I need you to find out what."

"I was already doing that. Why the need for all this secrecy."

"Do you now read the news, Bruce?" says Moira.

"Of course I do. Media backlash- whatever. Anthony, you shouldn't be letting this get to you. It's normal."

"Not this," says Anthony. "And we need to start fighting fire with fire. Look both; I know this isn't in your job role, so you can refuse me if you're not comfortable."

Both of them tense up, sharing a worried glance. They look like two people about to be sent to war. *Perhaps that's what they are*, thinks Anthony grimly. "I need you two to research dirt on Chambers and Chambers Energy. If we're going to counter this media backlash, we can't play nice anymore. We need to prove this guy is corrupt and that he's into shady business practices. Or even things in his personal life that could get him arrested. Anything that limits his ability to keep criticizing us in public."

Bruce scoffs. "Everyone knows Chambers is corrupt."

"Sure. But no one ever proved it. That's what I need you two to do."

"I'm a programmer, Anthony. If you want to Google your mortal enemy, do it on your own time."

"I'll do it," says Moira. Anthony looks at her with a smile. Bruce gives her an incredulous look. Moira shrugs. "If LevelUp goes down, then our jobs go down with it. I believe that in the future you want to make Anthony, and I know you do, too, Bruce. Or you wouldn't be here."

Bruce makes a grumbling noise, but he doesn't argue anymore. Anthony smiles. That's as close as the man ever gets to really agreeing to anything.

"Thank you," says Anthony. "I'll meet with you both every day to discuss progress. Don't tell anyone what you're doing, of course."

"Except Denise, right?" says Moira.

A swirl of guilt rises in Anthony's chest at hearing Denise's name. "No, not Denise," he says. "Not this time. She's taking some time off, and I'm worried about her. We don't need to add this to her burden. Just talk to me, okay?"

"Of course, sir," says Moira.

"If you say so," says Bruce.

The two of them leave looking paler than when they entered. Anthony leans back in his Herman Miller chair and lets out a long sigh. He doesn't feel any better. Until they put a stop to Chambers, he doesn't think he will.

Chapter 3:

The Mole

The receptionist on the other side of the desk frowns at her computer screen. Her finger rolls madly on her mouse wheel, clicking as it does. Anthony takes a deep breath to help him maintain his calm. *It isn't her fault*, he says. But he's getting anxious. This is the third office that he visited that day, where he was going to pre-arranged meetings with investors. The first one was canceled before he arrived. The second ended in a matter of minutes, and the CEO he had been talking to seemed to be watching the clock the whole time.

"Mr. Rodriguez doesn't have any meetings with you on his calendar," she says eventually. "Are you sure you've got the right day?"

"I'm sure," says Anthony. He gets his phone out and starts flicking through his emails. He finds the invitation to the meeting and holds it up for her to see. "A meeting at one. We're supposed to be going for lunch."

"It isn't there anymore. He must have canceled it."

"He couldn't have told me?" The receptionist starts to look a little panicked. She's young, and her desk is a mess. *Perhaps she's new*, thinks Anthony. He softens his tone. "Is it possible that you could call up to him so we can get this cleared up?"

The receptionist looks at the phone as though it might jump up and bite her. "I've never called the CEO before," she says. "This is a very big company, Mr. Brown. I could put you in touch with my manager?"

"Please try Rodriguez. It's very important that I speak to him about a future partnership here."

He means it. Rodriguez is one of the biggest investors that he's had his eye on for a long time. The man owns a healthcare company that has various operations throughout the country. It was an industry that was integral to the success of LevelUp- if the app is going to have the maximum benefit for the maximum number of people, then it needs to inspire innovation in industries that have a direct impact on their well-being. Healthcare is key to that.

"You're the LevelUp guy, right?" says the receptionist, looking Anthony up and down. "I saw you on the news. You said you want to make life better for people. Do you think you will?"

"As long as I have people like Rodriguez on my side."

She considers this for just a moment more, then takes a deep breath. Then she picks up the phone and makes the call. Anthony stands there for a few minutes as she is passed from person to person. She keeps getting put on hold. Eventually, she has some success.

"Is that Mr. Rodriguez? There's a...yes, him. Are you able to speak to him?"

A long pause. Anthony feels his body start to tense up. But the receptionist hands over the phone. Anthony exhales deeply.

The voice on the other end of the line is deep and serious. It carries just the hint of a Latin accent. "Mr. Brown," he says. "I'm sorry I didn't warn you about our canceled meeting. There has been a lot of time pressure on me lately. I've been told I shouldn't speak to you."

"Told by who?"

"I can't tell you that. But no investors want to speak to you at the moment, Mr. Brown. Our interests simply don't align with yours."

There is a note to his voice that Anthony can't quite put his finger on for a moment. But then he realizes- Rodriguez almost sounds scared! For a man with such a powerful reputation, it was ludicrous to think he would be frightened of speaking to Anthony. *Unless...*

"Is Chambers threatening you, Mr. Rodriguez?"

"Watch yourself, Mr. Brown. Accusations have a lot of consequences."

The lines go dead. The receptionist looks bewildered. "How did it go?" she says.

"It didn't," says Anthony.

"Do you want me to arrange another meeting?"

"No. Thank you."

***

Anthony sits in the driving seat of his company car, but he doesn't turn on the engine. He just grips the steering wheel so hard that his knuckles start to turn white, looking up at the main office of Rodriguez Healthcare.

How many people does Chambers have influence over? He had always known the man was powerful, but he had never considered that he would be this much of a threat. Anthony can't help but wonder what it is he's started here. He wanted to change the world, but he didn't realize how furiously the world would fight back.

He wants to connect investment directly to the people. He isn't trying to replace the others at the top, as far as he sees it; he's only trying to provide them with opportunities for growth. This benefits everyone, doesn't it?

He supposes that he has always seen the good in the world- the potential for change. He is a businessman, not a military strategist. But now he feels like he is fighting a way- working against an enemy who seems to be already incredibly well-versed in shady business tactics. Anthony doesn't want to fight dirty. He just wants things to change. All of his meetings prior to the launch of LevelUP had suggested that was exactly what investors wanted as well.

A call on his phone distracts him. He looks at it at once, hoping to see Denise's name. Instead, it's Bruces. He sighs and takes the call.

"This had better not be a complaint, Bruce," he says. "I've not got the mental load for it."

"It's about company security."

Anthony sits up in the driving seat. His pulse quickens. "You're alone, right? No one else can hear this call?"

"Relax. Of course, I'm alone." Bruce exhales, clearly smoking. Bruce didn't usually smoke during the day- he did that in the mornings and evenings, before and after work. "I've not found anything on Chambers. Looking online, it's like the man has never said a bad word in his life."

"That's not why you're calling. Get on with it, Bruce."

"I think we have a mole. We've got to."

Anthony pinches the bridge of his nose. He's suspected it, of course. But he hadn't really been allowing himself to think about the possibility seriously. There's nothing that means more to him than the loyalty and dedication of his team. His company is built on trust- in every single post he's filled, he has made sure that the people are fully vetted. He has made them sign NDAs, and he's spent a lot of time asking them about their support for the mission of the company. He thought he had been thorough. He guesses he has not been thorough enough.

"The business plan you sent through to me to sign off managed to get out somehow. I've checked my own email account, and there is no sign of any hacking. But I've found another email on the company backlog. It looks as though it was sent from your own computer to an address I don't recognize."

"They've been on my computer?"

"Yep. I'm assuming you're not stupid enough to leave it unprotected?"

"I have a password. A password I thought only *I* knew."

"You've never had anyone read over your shoulder as you've typed it in?"

Anthony tries to think back. He can't think of any specific occasion, but he knows it's possible. It's the same password he uses when he accesses emails on his phone. He's been all over the office when he's looked at emails on his phone. He supposes anyone could have seen it.

"What's the unknown email address?" he says.

"It's internal, somehow. The person using it has tried to make it sound non-descript like it could really be part of the company. It just says "docadmin@nexcorp.com," But that isn't an address any of our actual administration staff use."

"Terminate it."

"No. We can't let the mole know we're on to them, Anthony- that's spy work one-oh-one. Now we know the email address we're using. I keep an eye on it, and we see what they send next and when."

"This isn't my area of expertise, Bruce. In truth, I'm overwhelmed."

"It's okay, Anthony. You're not alone on this." His voice sounds unusually soft and sympathetic. Perhaps the nicest that Bruce has ever sounded to him. The man must be worried- he very rarely drops his tough exterior. "You know you can trust me, right? And Moira? In fact, I can get you a list of names of people in this company you should trust. Everyone who works under me, for example-"

"I trust you, Bruce. You wouldn't be telling me this otherwise. Moira, I'd trust forever. As for anyone else. Well. How am I supposed to now?"

"Paranoia isn't going to help you."

"It isn't paranoia if there's a mole, Bruce. It's informed caution."

Bruce sighs, but he doesn't disagree with him. "You need to clear your meetings, Anthony. This needs all of our attention."

Anthony feels sick. He knows that Bruce is right, but it pains him so much to admit it. The meetings are integral for the next step for LevelUp, but they aren't getting him anywhere. If what Rodriguez said is true, then he knows that they're all going to just end up with more cancellations. More disinterested faces.

"I'll clear my schedule," he says. "Update Moira. And double down your efforts to find some dirt on Chambers. This is all connected, I know it."

"I've said already- he's squeaky clean."

"Keep looking."

Anthony ends the call. He looks at himself in the rearview mirror. There are dark bags under his eyes that he doesn't recognize. It's like he's looking at a man who's ten years older than him.

This can't go on forever, he asks himself. *Can it?*

***

When Anthony gets back to his office, he wastes no time at all opening up his computer. Denise isn't there to bring him lunch, and there's a clawing hunger in the pit of his stomach, but Anthony doesn't do anything about it. He can't do anything but concentrate on the problem at hand. The duel threat of factors that could bring down his company and choke his vision for the future- the threats of the mole and Chambers.

Bruce has already sent a list of staff names, with a line for each one commenting on the possibility that they are the mole. He's also included every single CV and job application they received from each one of those staff members. There are about twenty- most of the people who started at the company in the last couple of months.

Anthony opens the first one. Sara Walker, an administrator. She came straight from University to a poor family in the south. There's nothing suspicious there.

Yui Cheng- IT support. His CV is impressive, and prior to working for Anthony, he worked in hospitals up and down the country, keeping their life-saving systems active. Anthony can't suspect a man with such a positive background.

Asif Bekter. He's in marketing. Since starting at the company, he's created several great online ads that are plastered all over X and Facebook. Those adverts have led to a lot of downloads. It doesn't seem right that that guy would want to bring the company down.

Just a list of hardworking people, that's all that Anthony can see. He remembers each of the different applications that they sent in. They'd all impressed him in different ways.

He runs a hand through his hair. How is he supposed to sift through all of this? Unless one of those CVs has a direct link to Chambers, then what evidence does he have? He scrolls through each of them, and there is no mention anywhere of Chambers Energy or any of its subsidiaries. These are just perfectly normal job applications.

He racks his brains for what he can do next. How could he find out anymore? He considers the possibility of systematically interviewing staff, but what would he learn? The mole isn't going to just announce themselves. And Bruce is right; they don't want to alert the mole to their suspicions.

It seems like an impossible task. A task made even more impossible, combined with the fact that he's also trying to launch a world-changing app. He takes a brief look at the download report from sales. It's high-record breaking even- but lacking the momentum that Anthony expects. How long is it going to be until some of their pre-existing investors start to quit the platform? He can already imagine them now, receiving shady calls from Chambers and his cronies.

Three days. His app has been active for three days, and already he's worried about it falling apart. This isn't how it should be. This isn't what he's spent so much time working towards.

Anthony walks through the office with the intention of going outside to get some fresh air. When he walks through the workspaces, people smile, nod, say words of encouragement, and greet him. It's the same as always. But Anthony can't bring himself to return their smiles.

All he can think as he looks into each of their faces is, "Do I trust you?" He wonders how long he's going to have to wonder that for. He wonders when everything will get back on track.

***

Anthony sits in a bar, listening to the gentle prattling of the business lunches around him. It's a Friday. Most of them probably don't intend to do any more work today. And it's only two. He frowns. It isn't the work ethic he asks for from his own company. But what can he say? He's sat in a bar as well, and he is probably busier than anyone else there.

He isn't drinking- he won't, not even now, stressed as he is. He gave up alcohol in his uni days when he began to formulate his concept for LevelUp. Back then, it all seemed so simple. So clear. Everyone he spoke to thought he was mad, but they always agreed with him, ultimately.

Because Anthony knows how the world looks, capitalism was founded on innovation and competition. When you remember that, you start to see how the system operates- how people all rely on each other for new ideas and then build companies to experiment with those ideas in new and exciting ways that benefit society as a whole. To Anthony, it was the comfortable giants of industries that were the real enemies of business. Rather than experimenting, competing, and inspiring others, they hold on to their profits. They stamp out competition, buy it out, or discourage new research. They are like the dragons in fairytales- holding on to their treasure hoard, overwhelming any fresh-faced new adventurer who dared to try and take a little of those riches for themselves.

Anthony realizes he is learning that those giant, established companies are even more like dragons than he had once thought. These dragons have claws. They are cruel, and they have no problem at all with destroying their enemies entirely.

His phone rings. He ignores it. It buzzes. He sighs, sips his kombucha, and takes it out of his pocket.

There's a long line of text messages there- a mixture of messages from Moira and messages from Bruce. Not a single one from Denise. The latest text from Bruce includes a link. Anthony doesn't want to click on it.

Is this something bad? Anthony texts back.

It takes just a few seconds to get a reply. *Of course, it is. Everything's bad at the moment.*

I don't know how much more bad news I can take.

You can't bury your head in the sand, either. Where are you? I've been up to your office three times in the last hour.

Anthony doesn't reply to that. He opens the link that Bruce sent him. It takes him to the "Progress Conference" website. There, on the front page, is an article that makes his eyes open wide. He almost drops his drink in shock. He has to grip through reflex to keep hold of it, and some of it sloshes over his fingers and onto the bar.

"Watch it," says the barman.

Anthony ignores him.

The page is titled "NexCorp's Five-Year Plan: The End of American Corporate Freedom".

It has everything. Anthony plans to implement absolutely every change and move forward when the app starts to gain popularity.

He is planning to make business plans, and minutes from investor meetings and documents are available in the public domain. That plan is now public information.

He is planning to prioritize investment in poorer countries, connecting American investors with developing economies. That plan is now public information.

He is planning to create specific targeted groups of business innovators to challenge the position of long-established companies with damaging business practices. That's all public information as well.

None of those plans have been implemented yet. He didn't know if they were ever *going* to be implemented. They are just ideas- ideas that had been drawn up in office brainstorming sessions. Whether or not he is going to implement them depends heavily on the growth of the business and the public reception that he receives for his work.

All of that is now ruined. He is already being portrayed by the Progress Conference as an enemy of the American people. A quick internet search reveals that people are beginning to notice. There are forums that are alive with people outraged by the proposals. There are even conspiracy theories beginning to swirl- that Anthony works for the Chinese government. That his company intends to destroy American life.

All Anthony wants to do is make the world a better place. None of this represents his intentions. He was only ever going to make changes if it was clear that they were going to be popular- if they were clearly the things that society needs and wants.

He leaves the bar, stands out on the street, and takes a deep breath. He should head back to the office. But can he face his staff? How many of them have been taken in by all of this nonsense? And which of them can he really trust?

A man is standing outside, wearing a t-shirt with an American flag on it and shades that have a blue reflective surface. He is looking at his phone. He looks up and squints at Anthony.

"You're him, aren't you? The guy who wants to ruin our lives." He spits on the floor. "I never thought Green City could make a man like you."

"You can't trust everything you read online."

"Yeah? You talk like you know what we want, but that's a pretty classy joint you've just walked out from. I'd say you're out of touch." He scrunches up his face- an expression of disgust. "You should watch yourself, rich boy. People around here don't need you in our city."

Anthony heads back to the office, suddenly feeling unsafe. He can hear the jeering laugh of the man with the American flag shirt behind him. He just keeps walking.

He isn't sure if he can face anyone in the office, but he needs to be somewhere he knows. Somewhere where people aren't looking at him like he's an enemy.

Chambers is doing more than making him an enemy in business. Now, he's threatening to ruin Anthony's life. And Anthony isn't sure if he can take it.

***

Anthony walks through the workspaces, hardly looking at anyone. No one offered him a hello this time. When Anthony does dare glance on either side of him, he sees the pale faces of people who look physically sick and worried. Things are going downhill fast- faster than Anthony could have ever predicted.

He goes into his office and locks his door. He's never done that before. He's always tried to keep an open door policy, wanting his staff to feel like they can come and talk to him about anything- any problem, big or small.

Now, he doesn't want to hear any problems. He doesn't want to hear from anyone. His phone is buzzing constantly- calls from Moira, Bruce, and a dozen other department managers that he does not want to talk to.

No calls from Denise. Denise is the only one he wants to speak to, the only person who can ever calm him down. He can't bother her when she's sick, especially not if he's the one who caused her to stop coming in.

Anthony turns his phone off and puts it into a drawer. Finally, he has silence. He takes some deep breaths, practices mindfulness meditation, and clears his mind.

It's a difficult process, but he gets his breathing under control. The beginnings of a plan are already formulated in his mind. He needs to take proactive action- he needs to find allies, people who share his vision, and investors who really care about the future he's trying to create. He needs to connect with them to present a united front to the public. To tell them he cares about them. That he knows what he's doing, and he doesn't want to step on any of their freedoms.

His desk phone rings. For a few seconds, Anthony just stares at it. His desk phone never rings. Everyone in the office knows that they should call him on his mobile if they want to reach him. It isn't a number he recognizes.

This is going to be more bad news. He can feel it in his bones. But the angry man on the street was right. He can't keep burying his head in the sand any longer.

He takes the phone and holds it up to his ear. The voice on the other end of the line is nervous, not one he recognizes. It's an older woman, and her voice is croaky, perhaps from a lifetime spent smoking.

"Is that Mr. Brown?"

"How did you get this number?"

"Your receptionist put me through. I convinced her that I just wanted to help."

"I'm not sure who you are, lady, but no one can help me right now. I couldn't be busier. Please leave a message with the receptionist next time."

"I've got dirt on Chambers. The dirt you can use to bring him down. That doesn't interest you?"

Anthony's breath catches in his throat, and at once, he gets a note and a pen out from his desk drawer. "We'll meet up immediately," he says. "What's your address?"

Chapter 4:

Family Ties

Anthony can't quite believe what he's doing. Uber takes him out of town to the suburbs where he grew up, but he has never visited them since. Not since his parents passed away. Even when they were alive, he avoided the place as much as he could, coming just for Christmas and Birthdays.

His parents never quite believed in the mission that he was embarking on. His dad thought he was mad, putting ideology above profit. His Mom just wanted him to be happy and thought that Anthony was never quite happy. He never sought a family, and he never had any friends.

They never quite understood that the things that made him happy were working towards his dream. He never felt alive unless he was making plans for the future, helping ordinary people to bring their business dreams to life.

As the car drives on, Anthony feels a little more like himself again. He had been shocked; there was no doubt about that. But pressure is where he strives. He'd felt pressure before, back in the early days of NexCorp, when he had spent most of his time going from bank to bank, trying to get a loan to get the ball rolling. His dad never offered him a single cent for his ideas, and Anthony had never asked for it. Every bit of funding he ever received, he received off of his own back.

Anthony responds to the line of texts from different departments. He tells them to hang on- that they will find a way forward when he's free again, and they'll come up with a plan. He has no idea who he's about to go and meet. It could be a waste of time, but he's willing to follow any lead that he can get.

Still no text from Denise. *Give her her space*, he tells himself. There's no reason to stress her out more. He has no doubt that she's looking at the news right now, worrying the same as he is. Let her worry in her own way. It always took Denise time to process anxiety, but she always came back stronger when she was ready to start facing challenges again.

Anthony reminds himself that he isn't facing Chambers alone. He's still got his team with him. Even if he can't trust all of them, he knows his inner circle won't fail him. The first chance he gets, he's going to figure out a way around this problem. He's going to find a new idea, and he's going to get LevelUp back on track, fighting through the media storm of negative press.

***

The car stops at a run-down-looking place in a neighborhood that Anthony doesn't recognize. The Uber driver keeps looking ahead, tutting, like he's anxious to leave.

"Somewhere to be?" Anthony asks him.

"Anywhere but here," says the driver. "You from around here? No, wait, of course not. Look at your fancy suit."

Anthony looks down at himself, then around at his surroundings. There are high chain-link fences surrounding the yards of the houses around them. Outside of one is a woman smoking, with the glazed-over eyes of a drug addict. There are men coming towards him from the other end of the street, with a mean-looking dog at the end of a chain.

This *is* a rough-looking place. A victimized neighborhood- a result of the huge wealth disparity in Green City. He could practically smell the angst. He could practically feel the cutting impact of the dirty looks he was getting from the locals for daring to turn up wearing the uniform of the elite.

"You want some advice, pal? Keep that watch hidden," says the driver. "And book a cab to meet you right here when it's time to leave."

"I'll give you cash right now if you wait for me."

"Sorry, mister. I've got a wife that wants me home."

With that, the Uber speeds off. Anthony turns and approaches the house straight away before the hooded guys can catch up to him. He knocks and barely has his hand left the front of the door when it opens.

"Come on in," says the woman. The same voice from the phone. The place reeks of cigarettes, explaining her husky voice.

He steps into the house, and she closes the door behind them, double-bolting it. Anthony follows her through the hallway and into the lounge, where the smoke smell is strongest. The curtains are practically yellow from tobacco stains.

The woman herself looks old, but Anthony expects she isn't as old as she looks. Maybe she's sixty, sixty-five at most? She has the tired, strained face of someone who's had a damned hard life. As far as Anthony can tell, she lives alone.

"You still don't recognize me, do you?" she says. "It's Gloria. Aunt Gloria."

"My parents never mentioned any siblings."

"Of course not. Never had any time for family, did they? Well, last time I saw you, you were this high."

She makes a gesture with her hand, raising it a few feet off the ground. She smiles as she does it, and a hint of joy breaks through. There is a twinkle in her tired, old blue eyes that perhaps Anthony does recognize slightly. On the fringes of some childhood memory, somewhere.

Gloria leans back in her chair. She lights up a cigarette but puts it out again when she sees Anthony suppress a cough. She smiles apologetically. "Sorry. Not used to company."

"Aunt Gloria," says Anthony. The term feels odd coming off his tongue. He hasn't had anything resembling a family in a long time. "I appreciate you inviting me down. But this is a really crucial time for me, and my office is expecting me back."

She grins. "Just like your father. My brother. All business."

"I'm nothing like my father."

"No, you're not. Not in the ways that matter." She clears her throat. A rasping action that seems to take a lot of effort from her. "I've been reading about you a lot in the news, kid. I always knew you'd grow up to be something special, but I didn't realize you had an idea that could be so good for people. People like me. It sounds like you want to change this city. Change this world even."

Anthony nods. "Once this mess is cleared up with Chambers, yes. What's this dirt you have on him?"

Gloria hands him over a newspaper. It's old, faded, almost yellow. There's an article there titled "Nigel Brown in Hot Water. Brown Waste Management Under Investigation Over Hush Money Accusations."

He scans the article. He vaguely remembers the company from his childhood. It was one of many that his father ran. He can't remember the scandal being described, though. It seems as though the company was dumping people's waste in public waterways and had been accused of paying off city officials in order to get away with it.

Nothing ever proved, though. His father was accused of lots of different scandals over the years, and he was always good at covering them up.

"I know all about my father," says Brown. "His dodgy dealings were one of the reasons that I started Nexcorp. I knew I never wanted to be like him. But I don't see what this has to do with Chambers."

"Read it again, kid. I know you're a busy man, but try to actually read it instead of scanning it."

Anthony frowns- he isn't used to being told what to do. But he rereads the page. This time, a detail jumps out that widens his eyes.

The accusations of the hush money payments were released by Brown's business partner, Robert Chambers. Chambers (22) states, "I never knew a thing about it.

Of course, I was shocked. My family legacy has always been an honorable one, and I hate the idea of this besmirching my good name. Rest assured, I will be closing the company the first chance I get.

"He's a slippery bastard, that Chambers," says Gloria. "Your father found out he had been stealing money from the company, using a business account to pay for his luxury lifestyle. When your father threatened to turn him to the police, Chambers turned on him, sending this story to the paper. It turns out Chambers has a lot of friends in the media."

Of course he does, thought Anthony. It's the same right now. As soon as something starts going the wrong way, he sends messages to every reporter that he knows. That's how he's shutting down Anthony. It's why such a negative message about NexCorp was spread so quickly.

"Tell me what happened."

Gloria shrugs. "They decided to call it quits. Your dad dropped the robbery accusations, and in return, Chambers got his media dogs to stand down and drop the story. They covered up the evidence of the water dumping and quietly closed the company down. Your dad never was quite the same after that. He got more ruthless."

Anthony rereads the article, taking it all in. His eyes linger on the black and white photo of his father, a dozen microphones being shoved in the man's face. He really did look like Anthony. How could a man so different to him, be so similar?

Anthony vowed a long time ago to never be like the man who raised him. He renews that vow to himself now, in his own head. He stands.

"This has been interesting, Gloria, and I'll stay in touch. But it doesn't change anything- none of this proves that Chambers has done anything wrong. It's just more proof of how good he is at covering things up."

"I've got proof, kid. Don't worry about that. I have a file filled with his old bank statements, outlining every penny he ever took from that company and several others as well." She grins. "And I'm going to give you all of them. I just want something small in return."

"I know how to do a deal, Aunt Gloria."

"He can never know it was me. And you make sure he stops doing all of this twisted business stuff. I can't just watch him do this stuff anymore. It's making the world a worse place for everyone."

Anthony puts a hand on her shoulder to comfort her. He barely knows the woman, and it feels a little awkward, but if what she's saying is true, then that made her family. Possibly the only family that Anthony has left. And he knows he has to respect that.

Gloria's smile warms at his touch. She hobbles to her feet and then leads him through the tiny house.

They stop outside of a room that seems like it hasn't been touched since the 1990s. There's a computer there wide enough to use as a battering ram, a desk phone with a long curly wire, and a smell to the place like old ink and mothballs. Gloria opens a drawer in a filing cabinet, pulling out a thick file. She hands it straight to Anthony, and Anthony takes it willingly.

"Gloria, how do you have all of this stuff?" he asks. "This doesn't make any sense."

"You really don't remember, do you? You think that all of this stuff is business. It's much more than that."

"What are you talking about?"

"My name is Gloria Chambers, kid. I'm Robert's stepmom. And he's your cousin."

***

They go back to Gloria's lounge. Anthony still can't quite believe what he's hearing. It's like his past has all been a lie. He had never been close with his family- his father and mother had always been cool and distant- but they still could have told him some of this, couldn't they?

Browns keep their skeletons hidden, his father had always said. *It isn't good for businesses to parade our dirty laundry in public.*

Anthony supposes that all of this counted as dirty laundry in his father's eyes.

Gloria makes them both a cup of coffee, and Anthony is too deep in thought to remember to tell her that he doesn't drink it. He expects that Gloria isn't really the type of woman to care about what her guests want, anyway.

"You look like you've just seen a murder, kid," she says. "To me, all of this is ancient history."

"To me, it is now very relevant," says Anthony. "I need you to tell me everything, Aunt Gloria."

"I don't really want to drag up the past. I only invited you here to give you the dirt to take down my stepson."

"Please. Anything you can tell me is important for the future of my business. I need to know what Chambers knows. I need to know why he has such an intense personal vendetta against me and my ideas."

Gloria sighs, then shrugs. She doesn't turn the TV off, but she turns the volume right down. Her eyes never leave the football game that's on, even when she's talking.

"Gordon- that's Robert's father- never did get on with marriage. Same as Robert, from what I've heard. I was Gordon's second woman. He came to me when he was bored. He took me to fancy meals and dressed me up in expensive dresses. I'd never seen much of the high life. He dazzled me with it; what can I say? I didn't know he was married. Not to start with, anyway. When I eventually found out, he made me feel like I couldn't break it off. He was a charmer, even though he wasn't a looker."

"Sounds familiar," mutters Anthony to himself. He's thinking back to the teenage Robert Chambers, who always seemed to have a parade of girls following him.

"Believe it or not, kid, I was a looker back in the day. Cigarettes ruin a pretty face." She takes a long drag on the one she's holding. "I could have had a dozen men- good guys as well. But none of them had

Gordon's money. We had a kid together. My daughter, Britney. Not sure where she is now. He gave me thousands and thousands of dollars in return for me keeping Britney a secret. Gordon's never met her. Britney doesn't want to meet him."

A cousin, Anthony thought. His family was growing by the second.

"Gordon's wife found out he was having an affair. She kicked him out for a while, and he came to live here. He hated it, of course. This run-down neighborhood was beneath him, and he got out as soon as he could, finding some other, more wealthy lady to meet up with. I was heartbroken." Her eyes are glassy. Anthony doubts the hard old woman is capable of properly crying, but he can still see the hurt and upset in her eyes. "I never really got over it. His parting gift to me was dumping his kid on me. Robert was ten at the time, and he called me stepmother. I had to raise him up until he was a grown man. Neither of us saw Gordon again.

"Robert hated it here. He didn't have much physical money to his name, but he knew he was due a fortune one day from his inheritance. His dad was still sending him money as well. Thousands every month, from what I heard. Not that I saw a penny of it. I was still cooking dinner for him, even when he had enough money to go out and eat at fancy restaurants every night. When he started his first business, he kept on living here. That room you were just in, that was his study. He kept every document in there. Including details of his business dealings that were damned shady."

Even though he had only met her a short while ago, Anthony felt a rush of anger thinking about how Robert had taken advantage of his aunt. He could have given her a share of his fortune- could have gotten her out of this rough neighborhood after all she had done for him. Instead, he lived with her as long as he could, using her place as a free office. And then he never even bothered to move his stuff out when he eventually left.

"It sounds like he took over your life."

Gloria shrugs. "He was family. Not that he ever acted like it. Besides, a childhood being raised by his father had started to turn him into a selfish little monster. I wanted to try and change that, but it never did any good.

"It was through me that he met your father. Nigel didn't visit often, but when he did, he spent more time talking to Robert than he did to me. They had a shared interest in building businesses and trying to get rich. Robert convinced him to go into business together. He rubbed off on your father. Turned him from a respectable businessman into a ruthless, profit-driven monster."

"And I was a teenage kid," says Anthony. "At boarding school, completely oblivious to all of this happening."

"I guess so. But looks like things have turned out alright for you." Gloria's eyes are bright and intelligent, even if they have been dulled by time. She looks Anthony up and down as though she's analyzing him. "You know, you remind me of your father, kid. Not as he was, but how he started. You need to be careful. Business changes people. I saw it happen to too many people in my life. You get a whiff of that good money, and you start to want more of it." She sighs. "Not that I can blame people. I never cared about money and always tried to do the right thing. Look at me now, still stuck in this neighborhood."

"You haven't been treated right," says Anthony. "Look, Gloria, you've given me these files, and they might really help me. If I could help you as well..."

"I ain't no charity case, kid. Just an old woman with a hell of a lot of bitter feelings rumbling around my head. Do you want to do something for me? You use those files to stop Robert in his tracks. You do what you say you're gonna do. Make the world better for people who live like me."

Anthony stands. "I promise I will, Aunt Gloria."

"I've heard that before. Good luck, kid."

He calls another Uber and waits on Gloria's porch for it to arrive. He ignores the shifty glances from the people who pass by.

Now that he's got time to properly process the place, he can see what a rough place this is. There are smashed windows up and down the street. There are endless cigarette butts on the floor, as well as needles. As he waits, he hears an argument echoing from a few doors down. A man and a woman, threatening violence on one another.

Even in that rough place, Anthony is sure that there have to be good ideas somewhere. LevelUp is exactly what this place needs- providing a route for anyone to break out of poverty. It reinforces to him the importance of his mission. The importance of fighting against Chambers's efforts to destroy him is to make sure that he comes out on top.

His car arrives, and Anthony gets in. As they drive, he looks out the window over at the corporate center of the city that swells into view, filled with skyscrapers and swanky bars. The juxtaposition between the rich city center and the rough neighborhood he just left is stark. It almost makes him feel embarrassed. He had always known that he was privileged to live in the affluent areas of the city, but he hadn't realized quite how lucky he really was.

It's starting to rain, and there are dark clouds in the sky. But it's still clear enough for him to look across Green City and see the looming, towering building that was the corporate headquarters of Chambers Energy.

His nemesis is there. He sees that now. Chambers is more than just a rival. He's been involved throughout Anthony's life, pulling the strings.

But Anthony has a file that might just finally bring him down.

***

The Uber drive back to the office seems to take a lot longer than the drive to Gloria's house. Anthony feels as though he's just had his life turned upside down. He never thought he could learn so much about himself and his past in so short a space of time. His father had never really talked about family. Anthony had always presumed that there wasn't much to know. How had he taken this long to find out?

He's ready to fight, and now it's personal. Anthony doesn't intend to pull any more punches. Chambers has been going on the offensive, and now it is Anthony's turn to do the same.

When he gets to the office, Anthony walks personally into every single workspace. He summons managers directly, getting them to follow him in a line as he musters every single important figure involved in NexCorp. Then he leads them straight to the boardroom, closes the door, and turns the lights on.

There's a buzz of panic and excitement in the room. This is the first time that most of them have seen Anthony since Chambers's scathing article dropped just the day before. Anthony is sure they have all assumed that he was licking his wounds, hiding.

But Anthony isn't going to hide anymore. Not with so many personal stakes in this long-term betrayal.

"Quiet, everyone," he says. "Chambers Energy has declared war on us. This is no longer a boardroom. This is a war room, and I want everyone on my side. We are going to meet back here every single day and discuss our ideas. We are going to beat this negative press. We are going to keep LevelUp running exactly as planned. I need ideas and people, and I need action." He pulls a whiteboard out for everyone to see. "Who wants to begin?"

Chapter 5:

Corporate Espionage

The boardroom meetings start off with a slow momentum. Anthony finds himself having to change the mindset of the people who are working for him. So many of them have been reading the news and making preconceived ideas that the company, the idea, and the dream were already dead in the water. Destroyed before they ever had a chance to truly begin to grow.

Anthony has a policy in every single one of those daily meetings. Any talk of defeat, giving in, or scaling back operations is completely banned. Anyone who suggests anything like it is told to start thinking of a different idea. He can see the frustration on people's faces. He can see hopelessness, and he can even see the beginnings of resentment. But Anthony is like a man possessed now. He spends every waking moment of his day planning and strategizing how he's going to take down Chambers. How he's going to choke out this public slandering of the new service he's going to make?

Whenever he wakes up, whenever he's completing his morning exercises, he keeps the image of the world he wants in his head. He's manifesting his success, picturing himself shaking hands with business leaders and world leaders. He's imagining LevelUp finding its way across the entire globe. He pictures a man in the poorest parts of India who is just as able to bring an idea to life as any wealthy guy in the States. Access to good funding won't be a limitation any more. The only limitation will be the imagination of people and the selfishness that makes them resistant to change.

***

As Anthony steps into the office, he is accosted by a man he knows but doesn't deal with often. He is in charge of financing and budget- a pen-pushing type called Harvey Wilter.

"Sir, I really need to speak to you about the budget."

"You can book a meeting, Harvey."

"I tried to raise it in the last boardroom you called."

"The boardroom is for strategizing and survival. It's where we talk about how we're going to take down Chambers and secure our futures. It isn't for talks about which pot of money goes where."

"Sir, please can we take a private office." Harvey is keeping his voice low, whispering so others can't hear him, but at some of the desks they walk past, people are starting to look up. Anthony has a moment of realization of how this probably looks to the rest of them. Here is a staff member of his trying to come to him with a genuine concern, and Anthony is shutting him down.

Anthony feels a little embarrassed. If he is honest with himself, this kind of thing is usually Denise's domain. But she hasn't been in for a week now and doesn't show any signs of changing that. He needs to take charge of more around here. He has to take ownership and responsibility for all of NexCorp since he can't rely on others to do that for him.

"Sorry, Harvey. Come with me."

He sits Harvey down in his office and takes the time to make him a cup of coffee. He doesn't drink it, but Denise makes sure that he keeps a Nespresso machine on his desk so that he has something to offer the clients who visit him. Harvey takes the coffee willingly, looking a little more relaxed now.

Good, Anthony thinks. He needs his top staff relaxed if he's going to get them talking, thinking, and planning for the future.

"What's this all about?" Anthony says. "I understand that the budget is important, but I'm trying to keep a long-term perspective on things at the moment."

Harvey looks down at his feet. He pushes his spectacles up the bridge of his nose. His cheeks have gone a bit red- another anxious guy. But, according to Denise, he did a great job of keeping their finances on track. *I really should get to know these people more,* Anthony thinks.

"That's exactly it, sir," says Harvey, still not meeting Anthony's eye. "Long term, there just isn't going to *be* a budget if we keep on going as we are. When LevelUp first launched, we received lots of advertising revenue from businesses looking to succeed through the platform. But now they just aren't coming to us in the numbers we want."

Anthony blinks at him. "But we're gaining users, not losing them, Harvey. We need to talk to the users that we have and get more of them on board."

"Yes. No. Well, that's the problem, sir. Our service is free- trust me, I understand why, and I think it's a great thing- but that means we have a lot of passive users. Lots of people who have business ideas are listing them on the app because it doesn't cost them anything. But they aren't trying to promote themselves. They don't want to hand money over to us because of a lot of them. Well, here are the user surveys we're sending out. They aren't promising."

"Talk straight to me, Harvey."

"People are frightened of our service, sir. They've read the news, but they might not all understand economics. But when the news is telling them that they should be scared, a lot of people can't help but listen."

Anthony sighs. *Scared.* What are people afraid of? Having access to more money? Having the chance of their dreams- to bring their ideas to life?

He tells himself that he can't blame them. Of course, they're listening to the news. Chambers hasn't exactly been quiet. In fact, he's been appearing on every TV or radio show that can tolerate him, and he's been picking holes in pretty much every part of NexCorp's plans for the future.

"We're going to beat him," Anthony says. "We're going to put a stop to this soon."

"The budgets are overrunning, sir. You're putting money into media and PR, and that money has to come from somewhere. Anyone looking at our accounts would come to the same conclusion- NexCorp is on its way to bankruptcy. We need to think about measures. Redundancies. Or even going public, selling off shares of the business."

Anthony shakes his head. "Both unacceptable options. Give me something realistic."

"This *is* reality, sir. Businesses need money to work. You know that as well as I do."

Anthony leans back in his office chair, staring at a blank space on the wall, the cogs of his mind whirring at speed. Of course, he knows that. He supposes he's been so used to avid investment over the last year or so. NexCorp has been building momentum ludicrously quickly, and he hasn't had to think about money for a while.

In his head, it had been such a straight path. Every forecast, every bit of market research he'd done, suggested that the money would keep coming. They didn't need reams of it- just enough to keep the business alive. He wasn't interested in growing profits as long as the service they were providing worked for people.

But he hadn't planned for Chambers. It was an oversight and one he feels damned foolish now for ignoring.

"Tell me, Harvey," he says. "If we keep our business model exactly the same, if we don't change a thing, how long do we have before we have to seriously consider bankruptcy?"

"Perhaps two or three months, sir. Soon enough, we should be helping people look for new jobs in preparation for closing."

"Not yet. I'm pouring all of my personal funds- all of the money my father left me- into the remainder of NexCorp. I'm going to buy us more time. We have to stay alive. For society, Harvey, you understand?"

"I'm trying to understand sir."

"Just keep me posted. And come to me anytime, okay? I'm sorry about before."

Harvey smiles and accepts the apology. He leaves the room not exactly looking confident but a lot less tense than when he entered. Anthony feels good- as though he's in a bit more control. He always thought that it was beneficial to him to let Denise handle a lot of the business communication, but he sees now how beneficial it can be to have more of a direct handle on it. He needs to know how his other departments are fairing- especially during this incredibly difficult time for the business.

***

The boardroom that afternoon has a different energy than the past few. People are talking excitedly. When Anthony asks for ideas, Moira stands up at once. She takes the floor at the front of the room with the confident brashness of a powerful executive.

"We're working tirelessly on getting people on our side," she says. "I've managed to get a panel of investors together who have agreed to take on a public forum, answering questions from concerned people live at the Exhibition Center at the exit of town."

Harvey raises a hand shyly. Moira raises her eyebrows at him, inviting him to speak. "The exhibition center isn't cheap," he says. "Are we paying for drinks for people? Food? How formal is this event?"

"Not formal at all," says Moira. "We want anyone to feel welcome, and we will be offering free tickets to get inside at the door. You don't need to worry about budget, Harvey. We aren't paying a single penny for this."

Anthony can't help but raise his eyebrows at that. "Not a cent?" he says. "I didn't realize we had such generous people left. Who's sponsoring us?"

Moira smiles at him. "Rodriguez Healthcare," she says.

Anthony can't help but laugh and clap. As soon as he starts, the whole boardroom explodes in applause. It's the perfect investor- a company with an incredibly positive public image that provides access to healthcare for thousands of desperate people.

But he remembers the last time he was in their office show, Mr. Rodriguez sounded almost frightened, even when talking to him. "How did you do it, Moira, you little miracle worker?"

She makes a mock shrug, smirking. "I guess some of us are blessed with the gift of charm. It also helped that I didn't tell him who I worked for. Not at first, at least, anyway. When he found out, he tried to turn the phone down, but I relayed the important message to him. I convinced him that investing in NexCorp would help hundreds of new innovative healthcare businesses start, and lots more people would get to live longer happier lives. It seems that was quite difficult for him to argue with."

More applause, even some cheers. Anthony looks around, delighted. The positive energy in the room is so thick he can almost feel like he can reach out and touch it. It was the good news that all of them needed. Anthony stands up and mouths "thank you" to Moira.

"Just doing my job," Moira mouths back with a wink.

Anthony takes the floor again. People fall quiet at once, with a different energy this time. They're smiling, leaning forward, ready to hang on to whatever is about to come out of his mouth, confident now that they're sure it's going to be good news. Anthony doesn't intend to disappoint them.

"I'm going to handle the public Q and A personally," he says. "I need people to see who I am and what I stand for and realize that I'm not an enemy of the state or a communist. Moira, will you join me?"

"With pleasure, boss," says Moira.

More applause, more smiles. Anthony lets the boardroom fall into casual chat, allowing a break for all of them. He wants to get more work done and get more ideas on the table, but he recognizes the importance of letting this positive moment sit for a while. They need to celebrate their successes wherever they can, he realizes. It will make them more resilient to despair when the bad news eventually comes.

***

Anthony gets to the office early the next working day. He only needs to set foot in the building to realize that the bad news has just arrived. His receptionist is looking anxious, as though she's ready to tell him something.

"You've heard the news from upstairs, sir?" she says. "Investors have been booking meetings all day, wanting to know what's going on. It sounds like they're weighing up their options."

"I don't listen to the news, Annie. It doesn't really help me focus. But thank you for telling me." He knows Annie's name now. He's had to call her a lot the past few days to make sure that meetings are getting booked in in Denise's absence. She's a lovely girl, as it turns out. She has three kids, and she's looking to start her own business through LevelUp, offering tutoring services in arts and crafts to disadvantaged families. She has one of her homemade bracelets on right now- made of beads with a colorful butterfly hanging off of it.

Anthony goes upstairs. He smiles at everyone he passes, but he doesn't stop to chat. He goes straight to Moira's floor, and with just one gesture towards the quiet office spaces, she knows what he wants. She comes into a pod with him and sits down, opening her laptop, not waiting for any instructions.

"One of Chambers's subsidiaries, Forward Digital Thinking, has just announced a plan today to launch a rival app to ours," she says. "I've taken a look at it. It pretends to be an open investment app, but the model isn't anything like ours. In fact, it mostly seems to operate by encouraging consumers to pay a hefty monthly fee in order to get free 'business advice' from professionals."

"Professionals that live in Chambers's pocket?"

"Naturally, sir."

"And, naturally, that advice goes somewhere along the lines of 'stay out of our markets, get your own?'"

"Naturally."

Anthony stands up, ready to leave. "Thanks for filling me in," he says.

Moira frowns at him. "What are you planning to do about this?" she says. "Their downloads are going up fast. It's nothing compared to LevelUp's numbers, but people are taking an interest. Plus, he's managed to get some very influential business people talking down our service and talking up his."

"Let him try it, Moira. This is competition. It's what I'm here for."

"You can't be serious. Our strategy is to have no strategy. That's what you want me to tell the department?"

"You understand our message, right, Moira? I'm taking on these companies that like to feel as though they have no competition. I'm not a hypocrite. I'm not going to try to stamp out this new app just because it wants to compete with us. Let them compete. Our service speaks for itself."

"Our service isn't making much money."

"Just keep your eye on it."

Moira shakes her head, but at least she's smiling. "I can't say I've ever worked with anyone like you before, Anthony."

Anthony grins at her. "I'm going to try and take that as a compliment."

***

More days pass with more ideas until Anthony finds himself staring at a webcam, about to go live. Moira is just at the doorway of his office, an encouraging smile on her face. She's got a file filled with information in her hand, just in case Anthony gets some difficult questions from the public. He doesn't think he'll need it, but it's still comforting to have her there. Almost everything about his idea- about his vision for the future- is in his head.

Moira couldn't book the Conference Center straight away, so until then, they need more ways to get in touch with the public- to make sure that they have a message going out that counter the media storm being created by Chambers. It's a daunting prospect. Anthony does not have access to the Chambers resources or media contacts. What he does have, though, are good ideas and good intentions.

He stares at the webcam, looking at the countdown on his watch before he goes live. He's never used a streaming service like Twitch before, but Moira assures him it's the best way for him to reach an audience. He looks at the number of attendees going up and up constantly. They're breaking records already- with the numbers of people in the active audience past four million and counting.

Bruce is in another office in the building, managing the questions and making sure that only the most pertinent information gets filtered through to Anthony. He's told him not to pull any punches, though. He wants to answer any question that comes up, even if it's critical or absurd. He knows that among the people watching are going to be influential people- those who are going to pass his messages on to larger news organizations. This has to be a positive message. One that challenges the ridiculous accusations that Chambers is throwing out against him.

5, 4, 3, 2 1. Anthony wears a smile, keeps a measured exterior. He doesn't have to fake it. This is his idea, his passion, and his vision. He's always been a confident speaker, but he could talk to the entire world about LevelUp and the vision of NexCorp.

"Welcome to this live stream directly from NexCorp HQ, in Green City," he says to the world. "I'm not going to waste your time with a boring presentation or droll corporate speech. The truth is, there's been a lot of nonsense out there about who we are and what we stand for. I'm here to tell you that we stand for you- the people. I've only ever wanted to make society run better and smoother and to give people opportunities. LevelUp does that by connecting people- for free- to the resources they need to bring a business to life. So ask me anything. No question is off the table."

Bruce sends the first question through. *Sure, the millionaire businessman says he wants to help the rest of us. Why don't you start by handing out some of your money?*

Too personal? Bruce asks alongside the question.

Nothing is too personal today, Anthony replies to him.

Anthony reads the question aloud and then answers it. "I've had success in my life; I'm not going to pretend that I haven't. But I've also never received a penny from anyone. My father left me money when he passed away, and today was the first week that I ever touched that money. I put every single penny of it into NexCorp. I knew that if I didn't, then the business would go under."

Please don't talk about finances, says Bruce.

We're talking about everything today, Anthony says back.

Anthony glances quickly at the chat box for the stream. Some people are doubting the truth of what he says. "I'll publish my personal account information on the NexCorp website later if proof is needed. I'll just censor any identifying information."

That has a positive reaction. *Wow, a rich guy who's transparent about money. Guess there's a first time for everything,* writes someone. And other people agree with him.

The next question that Bruce sends through is less personal but still a scathing one. *How can you prove you're not a communist who wants to bring America down?*

"We are a business. We make a profit. We pay our workers, and we help other people get their own businesses started. We are not a threat to the country, and we don't have any secrets. Anything anyone wants to know about our company is public information. And if you want to know anything else, then I'm happy to answer right now."

If you are in the pocket of a foreign government, then you would keep that secret no matter what.

"What evidence would *you* need for me to prove that we are not in any way affiliated with a foreign government?"

I personally wouldn't believe a single thing that comes out of your company's office. Someone else would have to go in and take a look. At all of your accounts and everything. Someone non-biased.

"Chambers can come and look around here himself if he wants. And he can take photos. He can speak to whoever he wants to. We've got nothing to hide."

Why should we choose LevelUp over BusinessGuru?

Anthony assumes that BusinessGuru is the name of the Chambers's app. "Because we are free. And because we don't have connections to any big companies who want to protect their dominance over a particular field or industry. Unlike Chambers. No one has been able to prove anything about his shady business past. But carry out a search online. You can make up your own mind."

Each one of his answers has Moira opening her eyes wide in alarm. Bruce is sending him a string of messages.

You can't say that; it's slander.

You can't just invite people into our office.

What if we can't keep these promises in the future?

Anthony understands why they're concerned, but he isn't bothered in the least. He knows exactly what the future for NexCorp looks like, and he knows that he needs the trust of the public to make it happen. He's open and honest because he has nothing to be worried about and nothing to hide.

He can tell it's going well. The negative comments in the chat box start to disappear. It sounds like most people are starting to listen.

Chapter 6:

Betrayal Revealed

The next boardroom meeting is tense. Every single person in the room was watching Anthony's stream, and a lot of people were really wary about it. Anthony understands why. Most of them, most likely, have never had an experience like this in their working lives. Most employers kept a lot of smoke and mirrors from the public. Company secrets are protected ferociously. Anything that has the potential to damage profits is strictly forbidden.

He wants to lead by example. Anthony knows that business doesn't have to be that way. They can be open about their choices and their vision without upsetting people because nothing they're doing has any ill intention behind it.

"I'm going to let Moira take the floor today," he says as he stands in front of his most trusted team manager. "After the stream last night, we need to hear from someone who was not directly involved. So you know that I'm not sugarcoating the impact or making it sound more impressive than it was."

"But it was impressive," says Moira, standing and talking at once. Anthony sits back down, making sure he doesn't look too pleased. These people are concerned and wary, even in the face of success. He doesn't want to shake their insecurities in any way. "Every single piece of feedback I've read has praised our honesty. Even for those people who don't agree with the change we're making to big business. They are impressed that Anthony wore his heart on his sleeve."

"But how is it affecting our security?" asks Bruce. Naturally, the most critical person in the room on any occasion. The first to play devil's advocate. "Are more people on our website scouring our documents? People will be trying to pick holes in what Anthony has been saying, to find contradictions."

"Of course," says Moira. "There are still conspiracy theories, but there have been no huge bombshells. People have looked, and they've seen what Anthony is saying is true. There's nothing on our website that contradicts the message he's given."

"Time will tell. People won't be happy if we can't deliver on his promises. Plus, internal documents have been leaked before. Who's to say they won't be leaked again?"

"It's your job to stop that, Bruce."

"I'm doing what I can. No system is infallible."

Anthony clears his throat. Everyone looks his way, silent. The only sound in the room is the ticking of the clock on the wall. *They're still undecided*, Anthony realizes. They're all listening incredibly carefully to the debate, still trying to figure out if Anthony made the right move. Anthony wants them to make their own minds up. He's only going to state facts. "From tomorrow, I'm starting a new policy," he says. "There's going to be no such thing as internal documents- except for those that directly relate to staff member's personal information. All of the minutes taken in any meeting are going to be published. Every idea, every plan. It's all going to be accessible to the public."

Bruce looks at Anthony with his mouth hung open. "You can't be serious. You're opening us up to the invasion, Anthony. You're putting our company at risk!"

"I don't think I am," Anthony says calmly. "I think I'm giving the people what they need. But that's for you all to decide."

The boardroom goes quiet. Moira takes charge again before things start to go awkward. "All I can say," she says. "Is that BusinessGuru's downloads have slowed down considerably, and that LevelUp's are growing at a much faster rate. We've had more emails from companies and CEOs. People are willing to meet with Anthony again. And the media can't get enough of him. Thinks seem to be getting back on track as a result of what the boss has done. Who knows if the momentum will last? But my view is we need to have faith in our CEO- everything you see around you is possible because of his vision and his hard work. If we can trust him a little further, then we might just start to see him turning NexCorp's fortunes around."

There is a pause- a moment of reflection. Then there is applause. It's thunderous, shaking the room and table, and people start to laugh. Anthony looks around at his staff, at his most trusted helpers, and he smiles. A tear stings the corner of his eye, and he blinks it away. For once, he allows himself to wallow in it. To enjoy the praise. After a few confused seconds, Bruce even starts to applaud.

Anthony's people still trust him. As long as NexCorp holds itself together, then there's hope. I hope that they can overcome the obstacles and challenges that the Chambers is putting in the way.

Then Bruce stands whilst everyone is still talking and celebrating. He comes right to Anthony's side and leans down to whisper in his ear.

"We need to talk," he says. "Straight away. And in private."

"If you have any more concerns you want to share, you can share them with the room," says Anthony. "This is everyone's time, Bruce. We can hash it out personally later."

"It's not that. I've just had a notification come through. Anthony- I think we can find the mole."

Anthony's smile fades. His face goes hard, serious. He gets up at once, making his excuses. He knows this conversation with Bruce might just be the most important conversation of his entire business career.

***

He leads the way into his office. They make a brief stop in the I.T. department for Bruce to grab his laptop. He does so without saying a word, brushing off the questions from his staff. Once they reach Anthony's office, Bruce locks the door. He opens his laptop at once, and his fingers start to clack madly on the keys.

"An email left our servers during the boardroom meeting," he says. "About seven minutes ago. I've set up tracking software- we should be able to see what device it was sent from."

"It can't be anyone high up in the company. They were all in the meeting with us."

"Anything's possible, Anthony. They could have put a timer on the email to send when they thought we were distracted. Or they could be in cahoots with someone lower down the chain who is acting on their behalf. In fact,"-

Bruce's explanation goes dead. His face goes pale. There's something in his eyes close to panic- and Anthony's never seen that there before.

"What's going on, Bruce?"

"That can't be right. Let me check again."

More clicking on the keys. Anthony purses his lips, doing his best to be patient. He doesn't like being in the dark with anything to do with his company. But he knows better than to push Bruce when the man is in his flow, working his hardest.

"She's been making pains to encrypt it, but it's sloppy."

"Who's she?"

"I don't know how to tell you this, Anthony."

"Tell me how it is, Bruce."

"This email came from Denise Bloom's laptop. It's got company account information attached to it- and it's being sent to another email address that I don't recognize. It has to be external. This has to be the leak, Anthony. There's no other possibility."

Anthony feels as though he's been punched in the gut. Denise Bloom. Anthony had never had a long-term romantic partner, so Denise was the closest thing in his life to that. Someone who supports him. Who makes him feel better when he's stressed or feeling low?

But, of course, it added up. She's been ringing in sick for a week. Anthony had been trying not to think about it, but Denise was never able to give a straight explanation for why she'd been off work. There's been no doctor's note. No warning. No indication of when she's going to be back.

And now he knows why. Maybe it's guilt. Maybe it's because she's been planning to leave the company completely. Either way, she's betrayed him. *Denise Bloom has betrayed me.* Even thinking it feels ridiculous- so wild a statement as to almost be a paradox. Denise has been there since he left university. She was the first person ever listed as an employee of NexCorp. Dammit, she was the one who bought champagne to celebrate when Anthony secured his first office space.

They've gone to the gym together. Watched movies. Laughed and cried together. They're friends. Perhaps the only real friend that Anthony's ever known.

"There has to be an explanation for this," he says. "Maybe she's being framed. That's possible, isn't it?"

Bruce grimaces. "Possible, sure. For an I.T. wizard who knows everything about hacking a company system. But that isn't Denise, Anthony. I had to teach her how to work her email account. She's old school. And this is a sloppy attempt at a cover-up."

Anthony stands up, pulling on his coat. "I'm going to go and talk to her."

"We should be calling the police. What she's done is illegal."

"Not until she's had a chance to explain."

"You're not being realistic, Anthony. You can't ignore the truth of what's happened here, even if it's a hard pill to swallow."

But Anthony isn't listening to him. He's already leaving the office, pulling out his phone and making sure there's an Uber waiting outside. This mess has to be cleared up straight away.

He needs to have no doubt in his mind at all if he's going to accept what he's being told.

***

Anthony tells the driver to stop a block away from Denise's apartment. He needs some time to clear his head. Ever since he heard Bruce's evidence, his mind has been running on pure adrenaline. Just like it had been after he heard the truth about his family history from Gloria, it seems like everything he knows about his life is being questioned, one after another. It's the most important time in his career and his entire life. It's a lot to balance- his business life and these intense, personal discoveries.

It's pressure like he's never felt before. The ultimate test of his resolve. And it's a test he's planning to pass.

As he approaches Denise's apartment, he takes a deep breath. He wants his voice to be calm and even as he makes his accusation. He doesn't want to let his feelings get in the way of what needs to be said. He needs to hear the truth from Denise, laid out plainly and in her own words. It's only when he's heard it from her own mouth that he'll dare to accept it as fact.

There's an elevator that will take him to Denise's floor, but Anthony ignores it and takes the stairs. He takes them at a calm, measured pace, controlling his breathing. He puts himself in a leveled, controlled state. By the time he's reached Denise's door, he's ready. He doesn't hesitate- he knocks on it three times. Loudly, but not aggressively.

After the knocks, the building is eerily quiet for a few seconds. Then he hears some muffled voices coming from Denise's room. Two voices in different pitches- Anthony guesses that her new boyfriend is there. He didn't anticipate embarrassing her in front of someone else. Perhaps he can convince her to go somewhere for a coffee. Somewhere quiet, where they can talk about this calmly.

The door swings open. Anthony is hit at once by a familiar stench of aftershave that he can't place. It's a deep, brash, spiced, show-offy smell. It takes him a moment to process the figure in the doorway. It's a portly man, almost filling the frame, and he's grinning wildly.

"Hello, Little Tony," says Chambers. "I wondered if you might pop around eventually."

He's wearing a Kimono that barely covers his body. It's tied loosely with a belt, and Anthony can see more of his cousin's body than he would like to be able to see. But Chambers doesn't seem to care. He seems to be enjoying laying himself bare, as though it's a power play.

"You're Denise's boyfriend," says Anthony. A picture is becoming clear in his mind. Denise hadn't had to invite her boyfriend to the launch party because Anthony had already invited him. "I'm sure Mrs. Chambers would be delighted by this revelation."

"Mrs. Chambers knows that she doesn't get a say over what I do or where I go," says Chambers. "You've been enjoying my broadcasts? I've been enjoying yours. Quite the little celebrity you're making yourself."

"I'm here to see Denise."

"Obviously."

"Get her for me."

"I'm not doing anything for you, Little Tony. You've set out to destroy my life and my business, and I intend to return the favor before you get the chance."

There's a woman's gasp from the apartment. Denise has finally noticed him. Still grinning, Chambers steps aside so that he can see. Denise is there, wearing a kimono, just like Chambers. She stares at Anthony with wide eyes for just a second before she looks down at the ground, resigned.

"I knew this was coming. Give me a moment, Tony; I'll come and speak to you."

"I think Little Tony was just leaving, actually," says Chambers. "He's seen everything he needs to see."

"Get out of here, Robert. Right now."

Chambers scowls at her for a second, then shrugs. She goes over and kisses Denise. She doesn't look like she wants to. She looks embarrassed. But Chambers kisses her anyway. Dragging it out, Anthony presumes for his benefit.

Anthony doesn't react. It's a pathetic way to goad. Childish. He can see that Chambers hasn't changed at all from that mean little teenager he used to be. He's still a bully, and he's always going to be a bully.

They close the door to get changed. Anthony spends those minutes looking up at the ceiling, feeling numb. He can't even bring himself to be angry. The whole situation is so ridiculous, so hurtful, that he just feels sad. He considers leaving there and then. He's got the answers he wants; why is he hanging around?

He realizes it's because of Denise. The woman has been too big a part of his life. Anthony can't just let that go. He needs to have closure-even from a woman who has betrayed him totally.

When the door next opened, Chambers stood there in one of his brash blue suits. He pretends to tip a hat to Anthony, laughing. Then he walks down the corridor and gets into the lift, whistling cheerfully.

Denise is the next face to appear. She's been crying; that much is clear. Her cheeks are puffy, and her mascara has run down her face.

"Do you want to come in?" she says.

"That's the last thing I want to do," he says. "We can talk here. I don't plan on staying long."

"It isn't personal, Tony. You know that, don't you? Chambers is everything I need in a man. He's powerful. He makes me feel important."

"He's married."

Denise sighs. "I didn't say it wasn't complicated."

"I could call the police right now. They'd be here- corporate espionage is a crime, Denise."

"You could. But you won't. Even now, I know you won't do that to me, Tony. That's why it had to be me."

Anthony grimaces. She's right, dammit. He knows he can't do that to her, even now, even with everything she's done.

"You helped me start NexCorp. I thought you believed in it. How can you do this after everything we've been through? Don't you believe in the future anymore?"

"Robert helped me realize it. You're living in a dream world. People like him always come out on top. They know what's best for people, even if sometimes they do things that seem harmful. Big Business is king. It's always going to be king."

"I presume he's paid you."

"More than you could have ever offered me."

"I gave you double what any other P.A. would get."

"And you still never respected my opinions. You always put too much on my plate and just expected me to do things." She opens her arms up. "I guess this is what happens. Let this be a lesson for the future."

Anthony walks away. It's too much to hear Denise's twisted logic. He knows he's been there for her in the past. He's held her hand when she's gone through divorces. He's calmed her down throughout her history of anxiety and mental health. Yes, he's worked her hard. He knows he can be pig-headed at times- so focused on the future that he forgets to act rationally in the present. But this, the attempted destruction of his dream, is not an acceptable punishment for that.

She could have just talked to him. Why couldn't she have talked to him?

"Tony," says Denise from behind him.

Tony keeps on walking.

"Tony!"

Now she's shouting. Tony hears her footsteps behind him. He doesn't slow down, but he doesn't speed up either. He keeps walking forward at the same purposeful, measured pace. Denise is struggling to keep up with him. She's waving something in his face- a USB drive.

"Take this with you," she says. "It's too late to stop what's to come, but at least you can be prepared for it."

"I don't need anything more from you, Denise."

"NexCorp is finished. There's nothing more you can do to stop it. Robert's got it all planned out. You deserve to know the truth."

Tony takes the USB drive. Mainly just to stop her from following him. She turns around, and Tony can hear her shuffling away. He expects it's the last time he'll ever see her, and looking back is too painful.

When he's out the stairs, he makes his way across the car park towards the taxi that's waiting for him. He keeps on looking forward like he's always done, like he always intends to do.

He doesn't care what Chambers has planned. He isn't going to let him win. Not while he still has his fighting spirit and an office filled with people he can trust who will fight on his side no matter what.

***

When he gets back to the office, Anthony doesn't waste any time. He gets Moira and Bruce together, and they go up to his office. He feels that he can trust them more than anyone now. Not having Denise around has been helpful in one way- it's taught him that he needs to include more people in his inner circle. People with specific skill sets who can creatively solve problems.

He is sick of working under tense, strained conditions. He allows himself a moment of peace and has Annie bring them up for lunch. She brings them warm pastries straight from the beloved bakery opposite the office when the room is filled with the smell of fresh baking and alive with the sounds of happy munching, it's hard to feel as stressed.

He still has his team. He still has his future. Denise is gone, but she wasn't everything to him. It just means he has to take more responsibility now- both for himself and the welfare of his staff.

"As much as I appreciate the once-in-a-lifetime meal offer, sir," says Moira. "I can't help but feel this is a little out of character. What's going on?"

"Denise was the Mole."

"Bruce told me." She shrugs. "It doesn't make much of a difference. The good thing is that we found it out."

It's hard for Antony to avoid smiling. Moira's positivity is powerful and infectious. It pays to have someone like that around- to put a spin on everything, to make it seem like an opportunity.

"She's claimed that Chambers has everything he needs to bring us down. And she gave me this." He holds out the USB stick for them all to see. "Maybe she's feeling guilty. Maybe it's a trick. She says that Chambers's plan is outlined on this thing and that there's nothing we can do to stop it."

"Don't you dare plug that into any company computer," says Bruce. He's frowning and serious, even when he has a mouth filled with warm apple pie.

"Relax. I have my own laptop here. It's connected to my personal mobile data, not the company Wi-Fi. There's no way for anything on this USB stick to touch our files. Right?"

Bruce nods, but he keeps on glaring at the USB stick as if it might jump up and bite him in the neck. Anthony smiles. He guesses it's not a bad thing to have a security whiz who's a little paranoid.

He plugs the drive into his computer, and inside is a single document. He opens it and sees that it's only four pages long. Each page is broken down into bullet points, detailing every step of the Chambers's plan to undermine NexCorp.

It seems as though most of the content in the first two pages has already taken place. They outline Chambers's media contacts and the stories he intends to leak to the press. There are comments about the documents that they got Denise to leak, which hurt Anthony, but he ignores them. He scrolls through to page three, which outlines the latest developments in Chambers's crusade. He reads through it with a furrowed brow.

"What?" says Bruce. "Is it bad?"

"According to this document, they've targeted our three biggest investors. Apparently, they're going to be contacting us any day now to tell us that they want to pull out. Chambers has offered them a lot of money to do so." Anthony exhales. "That's going to be a blow. At least twenty percent of the money we have available for new businesses."

Bruce looks furious at the news, his cheeks going red, the thick vein on his forehead swelling as though it's about to pop. "That's an outrage. Talk about disgusting business practices. It's malicious, is what it is. It doesn't have anything to do with Chambers Energy."

Moira just shrugs. "We lose investors, we get new ones. That's the way of the world. This isn't going to bring us."

Anthony nods, but he isn't sure, in truth. In his head, he is picturing the charts that Harvey sent him, outlining their rising costs against their funding. Investors are the key to making the service work, and they are already working to an incredibly tight margin as it is.

Keep looking forward, Anthony reminds himself. Denise and Chambers might be sure that they're going to destroy him, but they don't know the people that he has on his side. His team are the weapons in his arsenal, and he's going to keep on fighting with them all at his side.

Chapter 7:

Uncovering the Network

Anthony takes the information to the rest of the team. Not everybody receives it, including Moira or even Bruce. For many of them, Denise was a friend. Almost a mother figure in the office. People came to her with their personal problems, as well as their work problems. She was almost like the company spokesperson. The face that people saw most often, popping in and out of different departments.

"It doesn't matter," Anthony says. "This is a setback, but it doesn't change anything. We still have our plans and goals. We still have people on our side. Rodriguez is a great new business partner, and he's committed to being an investor. But we do have new enemies. We have to acknowledge that and accept it."

For once, Anthony puts a slide up on the digital screen behind him. He doesn't like PowerPoints, but he relents on this occasion. He wants people to know exactly who it is they're facing.

On the screen are three company logos. The "Big Three". Until yesterday, they had been some of their biggest investors. Now they were against NexCorp, in the pocket of Chambers, just like his sabotage plan had detailed.

There's Walker Solutions- a green energy company, and one of Chambers's own long-time rivals. Chambers must have paid Kelly Walker a hefty sum of money to get her allegiance. Anthony guesses that's just a sign of how frightened some big companies are of his ideas. They are even willing to turn enemies into allies to side against him.

The next logo is of Phillip Sterling- a huge bank organization that, until recently, catered only to the mega-wealthy, with a history of helping them avoid taxes. Anthony had thought that their signing on with

LevelUp was a sign that they were starting to change their ways. He guesses he had been giving them too much credit.

The third logo is a "Z" in a shaky, electric font. It stands for Z Inc.- a company at the forefront of AI development. Their new powerful support bot claims to be a tool for the public, one that can help them improve their writing and their employable skills to help them get better jobs and opportunities. Anthony heavily doubted their claims of selflessness. If they were in any way involved with Chambers, then it was clear that their priorities truly lay in maximizing income.

"Getting the "Big Three" on his side is Chambers's ace in the hole. He thinks that he's undermined us by buying them out, and- we have to be honest with ourselves- it has been damaging. They've already sent representatives to Chambers's conference panel. They've been all over the airways spreading absolute nonsense, trying to pick holes in the information I gave the public during my Q and A.

"As much as this is a setback, this is our chance to undermine these companies. By picking a side, they've shown that they don't care about ordinary people. If we can undermine them, then people will stop using their services. They will turn to their competitors- competitors that we're already approaching- and ask them to get involved in LevelUp. We've had a lot of interest. We need more ideas to find a way forward. Who has them?"

Anthony asks the question in a reflective silence. This is a big problem- probably more difficult than most of them are willing to try and tackle. Not when the stakes of using the wrong strategy are so high.

Normally, he would try a different strategy. He would get people to relax into the challenge, to give them the freedom to carry out reports and brainstorm a scatter-gun of ideas. But he doesn't have time for that anymore. Every day of work is crucial to the survival of NexCorp.

Harvey eventually raises a shaking hand. Anthony smiles at him, welcoming him to speak.

"You're talking about taking on other industries," he says. "Shouldn't we be focusing on ourselves? Trying to reduce our costs and plan for our futures?"

"No," says Moira. "The future of our business is dependent on other industries. We have to have an eye on everyone right now. It's a big job, but LevelUp is a revolutionary app. We're trying to change entire markets here."

Harvey grimaces. He won't say anymore out loud, but Anthony knows what he's thinking. They don't even know how long they can keep paying their own staff for, let alone worry about the future of three other businesses that have turned against them. But Anthony is determined to think outside the box. He knows that if he makes cuts now, then it will be the beginning of the end. The business will lose momentum, and LevelUp will be dead in the water.

No one else offers ideas, only questions. Anthony tries to belay their worries the best he can despite how frustrating it is.

"We're not getting anywhere," he says after an hour. "We'll meet again tomorrow, but I want an idea from every person here. Attract new investors in those three industries- that's the aim of the game. We need to consider everything and anything to make it work."

People leave, looking pale and shaky. Only Moira and Bruce stay behind. Moira looks completely unfazed, as though a good idea is going to just fall out of the sky any day now. Bruce looks like he hasn't been sleeping. There are dark bags under his eyes, and his pupils dart all around the place as though they're looking out for danger.

"This is getting big, Anthony," he says. "We're taking on giants here, and we're just a new startup. Sure, we're getting a lot of media attention, and we've grown quickly. But Chambers and his allies have been at the top of their industries for years. They control everything. It's putting the security of our company at risk."

"They aren't giants, Bruce, they're people," says Moira. "People have weaknesses, every single one of them. We'll come up with something, sir. I'll be working on it all night. And I'll meet with every team leader tomorrow to try and get something out of them."

Anthony puts a hand on both their shoulders. "I don't know what I'd do without you both," he says. "Truly and honestly."

***

"We believe what NexCorp are doing is un-American at best, completely illegal at worst," says the suit-clad man behind the podium. "No one asked Mr Brown if he could use our city for his little experiment. No one wants to see the collapse of the American economy right on their doorstep. I've been speaking to business experts from across this city, and they all agree that NexCorp is the enemy. During my next term in office, I will remove that enemy, one way or another."

Anthony straightens his back. He lifts the collar of his coat up and pushes his sunglasses further back onto his nose. He has no intention of being recognized. He's part of a crowd. He had to join it as soon as he saw that the rally was happening on the news. The Mayor of Green City is now preaching against NexCorp. A Mayor who, just a few months ago, was talking about the importance of reducing the wealth gap in the city.

Anthony had always assumed he would have a political ally in Mayor Arnold Stephens. He has met the man before, in the early days of NexCorp. The mayor had shaken his hand and told him emphatically that he believed in what Anthony was trying to do.

It's bizarre and disorienting to hear his name being used in a political speech. Even more bizarre are the cheers of agreement that the public has whenever Stevens drags his name a little further in the dirt.

"Another one to keep our eye on," says Moira, next to him.

Anthony sighs. There is a party-like atmosphere in the air. There's a stand nearby, deep-frying corn, dogs, and donuts. The air has the sickly sweet smell of a carnival. People are happy, laughing, cheering. Anthony feels like he's standing in a city he doesn't know. Stephens has always been popular throughout his time in office. Having his voice against theirs is a challenge he wasn't expecting to face.

"What the hell changed?" he mutters to Moira.

Moira shows him a list of donations on her phone. "He's been on the campaign trail."

Anthony scans it. At once, he sees the names of four companies that he knows all too well- Chambers Energy and the three businesses that he's charmed. The "Big Three" had been the biggest investors listed on NexCorp.

"I thought Stephens was better than this."

"Not everyone has the same attitude as you," says Moira.

"How he can sleep at night."

"People can convince themselves they're doing the right thing when there's money involved. You know how charming Chambers can be."

Anthony knows all too well. He'd charmed Denise, his business partners, and now even influential politicians. Perhaps men like Chambers ran the whole damned country in secret. Anthony turns to leave- he's seen enough. Now it's time to figure out what he's going to do about it.

As he turns, he comes face to face with a stocky guy with a mean look on his face.

"You're him, ain't you?" asks the stranger. "The communist."

He's not keeping his voice down. More people in the crowd start to turn their heads. Anthony looks at Moira, who mouths the word "lie!" at him. But lying isn't something that Anthony's ever been very good at. His one failing as a businessman.

"I am," he says. "I wanted to see what all the commotion was about. Now, I'll be going back to my office."

"You've got a lot of nerve coming around here, showing your face around people who don't trust you."

"With respect, sir, this is a public main street. I can be here if I want to."

"I should teach you a damned lesson, you communist."

The stocky guy bunches his hands up into fists. There's a circle surrounding them now- members of the public standing back to watch. They're quiet- no one seems willing to intervene. They aren't saying that they approve, but they're not stopping the guy, either.

Anthony looks the stranger up and down. He's sure that if they were to have a fight, then Anthony could come out on top. He spent a lot of his daily exercise routine working on how to get wiry, controlled muscle. But he's never been in a physical fight before. He's not that uncivilized. "I'll be leaving now, sir," he says. "Maybe you should stop drinking for today. I can smell it on your breath. Clearly, you're not completely in control of your actions if you think attacking a man in a crowded street is a good idea."

The man's face goes red. "You're a real piece of work, wise guy." He raises his fist like he's ready to swing.

It's then that someone steps out of the crowd. It's a woman- blond, probably in her early fifties. She's holding a kid's hand, and the kid looks terrified. "What the hell do you think you're doing?" she demands. "There are kids here, you idiot. Is that what this city's coming to? We're attacking people in the street now?"

"Ma'am, he started it," says the stocky guy. "This guy wants to ruin your kid's future."

"If you attack him, I'm calling the police."

The stocky guy stands down. People are shooting evil glances at the mother, but she ignores them. She comes right up to Anthony with a sympathetic look on her face. "You should get out of this crowd," she says. "Follow me. I'll keep the crowd off you."

"That's kind," says Moira. "But we can look after ourselves."

"Like hell, you can. You stand out like a sore thumb in those fancy suits. Come on, with me."

She pushes through the crowd without another word. Anthony shares a glance with Moira, who shrugs, and then they follow the woman. As Anthony pushes through the crowd, he can feel the heat and anger in some of the glares being thrown his way. He keeps his head up and is focused forward.

The mother doesn't stop until they're clear of the main street, on one of the side commercial blocks that the political rally hasn't quite reached. She checks if her kid is okay, and the kid looks shaken, but he isn't hurt. Then he turns to Anthony with the same worried look in her eyes.

"No offense, man, but you need to get your head screwed on tighter. This is the biggest collection of idiots I've ever seen, and I've lived in Green all my life."

"I've never had to worry about walking around the city before," says Anthony.

"Well, that's probably before you started preaching online, isn't it?" says the woman. It's mock criticism; her eyes are twinkling with amusement.

"Are things really so bad around here?" asks Moira. "I didn't know so many people in this city cared about companies like NexCorp."

"Stephen's is popular. A lot of people just go along with what he says. I did- until the last few days when he's been talking nonsense." She turns to Anthony again. "Mr Brown, I want you to know that I believe in what you're doing. Not just me, but near enough every sensible person I know. These people are the loud ones. Most of us aren't looking for a fight, just an easier life. Remember the silent majority, Mr Brown. Most of us still support you; we're just not the going-out-on-the-street-and-starting-drunk-fights-type."

She leaves, dragging her kid behind her. Anthony links after her. Other people who have overheard the conversation smile his way. Ordinary people- shop workers and office staff- are out on their lunch break.

"That gives me hope," says Moira. "I guess Chambers can kick up a lot of fuss online. Most people will make up their own minds, though."

"I hope so," says Anthony. "My message isn't going to change."

"Guess you'll need someone to start bringing your lunch to you every day. We can't risk our CEO ending up in some street brawl."

Anthony shakes his head. "If I can't face the general public, then I look out of touch. I'll still be going out whenever I want, Moira, don't worry about that."

"Geez, you stubborn. At least avoid the political rallies."

Anthony smirks at her. "Good advice. I'll follow it next time. But let's not forget who dragged us both out here."

"I guess we've both learned a lesson then. Come on, back to the office."

***

That afternoon, there is a sense of tension and finality to the boardroom meeting that Anthony organized. By now, everyone is aware of the pressure being placed on the company. Political involvement has changed things- his staff are starting to feel as though they are doing something crazy. Dangerous, even. He looks around the faces of his inner circle. Would any of them leave? He supposed he couldn't blame them. They've all joined him because they agreed with his cause, but ultimately, they are people with families. People are just trying to do their job, to give themselves and their loved ones good lives.

Perhaps he can turn it around. Moira claims that she has a new strategy that can help bring everything together. Anthony doesn't dare to hope too hard, but he trusts Moira. He's never heard her make a claim that she couldn't back up.

Everyone settles down inside the boardroom. The smell of strong coffee is in the air- the smell of an overworked, stressed workforce. Anthony can tell just with a glance at their faces that they're all nearing the end of their tether. He knows that if they don't get a good idea soon, then they might start looking elsewhere for work.

"Good morning everyone," he says. He kept his voice steady and even, projecting as much calm as he could. "I know you've all been working hard on your ideas. I also know that a lot of you have struggled to come up with anything. That's fine. I'm sorry for putting so much pressure on all of you. Moira's taken the ideas that you've had, and I know she's refined them into a strategy that she believes will work.

"I know most of you have focused on ways we can get our old investors back on our side by promoting our moral message and by pointing out how Chambers's business model does not match their ethos as companies. Moira believes that she has a way to do this."

A sea of faces, completely focused. They are looking for an answer, a lifeline. If anyone can deliver it, it's Moira.

Moira stands up and takes the floor. Like always, it's like there is no pressure at all resting on her shoulders. She looks just as comfortable as she would be standing in front of a group of close friends, talking to them.

"Thank you for all of your ideas," she says. "Seriously. I've heard a lot of different perspectives, and it's clear we need to work quickly and within the limits of our budget. My answer is pretty simple. We call Chambers and the "Big Three" investors in to make a deal."

There are worried glances in the office. Anthony frowns, wondering whether he should interrupt. He's open to any ideas that might help, but he wasn't expecting this. Moira understands the stakes. Surely she has to be joking?

"The deal will be on terms that's going to be attractive to them. We agree to limit the scope of our product, keeping it overseas and allowing them to carry on their local businesses unperturbed by a threat to their profits.

"But the goal won't be to actually make a deal. The goal will be to get the four of them around a boardroom table."

He frowns, but Anthony finds himself smiling. Of course, there's a twist. Moira's mind for strategy is like no one else's.

She clicks a button on her laptop, and a new screen comes up. It's a still from Walker Solution's website. It outlines a plan for expansion- a wind farm outside of the city, producing enough power to meet the needs of local people in a clean, sustainable way.

Next, she shows a still from Chambers Energy's website. It shows that he is planning to ramp up the operations at a coal plant, using cheap coal imported from China.

She shows a still from Phillip Sterling's website. It shows the largest loan they've given out to a different energy company altogether, one of Chambers's rivals.

Finally, she shows a screenshot of Z's website. They are planning to install new servers in the city- huge energy, guzzling machines that will require a complete expansion of local power in order to fund. They're exploring contracts with dozens of energy companies. Neither of them is Chambers or Walker Solutions.

"What's the point of all this, Moira?" asks Bruce eventually. They've been talking through the business plans of these different companies for nearly twenty minutes, and he's not the only one who's confused.

"The point is that our rivals are not really allies. They all have different interests that they will be competing over. Chambers might have been able to convince them to stand together for now in an attempt to bring down NexCorp. But the alliance between them is paper thin. From what I've been able to figure out, everyone knows that the top CEOs at each of the three companies can't stand Chambers. It must have been very difficult for him to bring them together. That means it will be just as easy for us to bring them apart.

"We get them all in a boardroom, and we highlight their differences. We get them arguing with each other and not trusting each other. We help them see that none of them can get what they want if they all intend to stick to their plans. We show them that LevelUp is the only real way forward- the only way through the division."

"That's a lot of hopeful thinking," says Bruce.

"We have to start being hopeful. There isn't time to strategize forever."

"We have to take the time to factor in how this deal affects our users," says Harvey. "If we cancel our American operations, we lose most of our advertisers."

"The deal isn't really a deal, Harvey. They won't take it. They'll be too busy turning on each other."

"It's combative," says another person.

"We're inviting the wolves to our door," says another.

"We're making enemies of the most powerful business people in this city."

Fear and panic- that's what Anthony sees. He stands up, and they fall silent. This is the time they need their CEO, he realizes. To unite them all towards a single strategy. "This is the best idea we have," he says. "It's a risk that NexCorp needs to take. And we'll get it done quickly. If it fails, we can meet again. If all of you lose faith in me after this, then we can talk about it. But we have to try. We have to trust Moira. She's never let us down before."

Silence.

"Arrange the meeting, Moira," says Anthony. "I'm going to go away now and plan exactly how we're going to handle this."

The boardroom meeting ends, and the tension in the air is thick. *It doesn't matter*, Anthony tells himself. The clock is running out. Either their strategy works, or they fail. There is no middle ground.

Chapter 8:

Showdown

Anthony realizes he has been staring at the number he entered into his phone for about five minutes. Even with his office window closed, he can hear the bustling activity of Green City outside. Sirens are blaring. People are shouting. Traffic moves along at a blistering pace, as it always does in the city.

The sounds of society. But what kind of society is it going to be moving forward? He feels the fate of every single person in the city resting on his shoulders. His idea- his dream- is to make life better for every single one of them. His dream has never felt like a burden before. It feels like a burden now. And a battle. Not once in his professional career can he remember wasting five minutes on anything. He doesn't put things off. He wanders head first into every boardroom, every meeting, and every challenge.

But this he does not want to face. It's like his pride has grown legs and is standing over him, gripping hard onto his shoulders and holding him back from taking the next step.

Across from him, Moira raises an eyebrow. She sips at her coffee elegantly and patiently.

"I can call him if it's easier," she says. "I understand there's history between you two."

"More history that you might be able to guess," says Anthony. "That's why it has to be me that calls him."

"Then it's better just to rip off the band-aid, sir."

Anthony realizes she's right. He takes a deep breath and taps on his phone screen to start the call.

It rings once. Twice. Three times. Anthony can smell the sweat forming on his own body, fighting through the aftershave. Chambers is making him wait. No surprises there.

The line rings for so long that Anthony almost hangs up, ready to think of another way of getting through to the man. But it stops ringing just as Andy is about to move on, and then a horrible, goading, low, rumbling voice echoes from the phone.

"Little Tony," says Robert Chambers. "I hadn't been expecting a personal call. I take it this means no hard feelings, then? About Denise, I mean."

"This is a business call."

"Then, really, it should go through my secretary. I could pass on her number?"

"Just listen, Chambers. I want to arrange a meeting. It's about time we cut a deal."

A pause. Anthony can hear a faint crackling noise- the sound of Chambers inhaling a cigar. Anthony can picture the man's face, broken into one of those mocking grins of his. "Ah, Little Tony, that's the most sensible thing I've heard you say in years. You must be really starting to mature. It's a cruel world, isn't it? I never wanted to ruin your ideas, my boy; I just want you to be realistic about some of the changes you want to make."

"Are you going to come or not? It's tomorrow. Later rather than earlier."

"I wouldn't miss it for the world. I'll be there at six."

"Good."

Anthony hangs up before Chambers can get another word in. He feels a little relief that the call is over, but not as much as he would like. This is just the first part of the plan. There's still a hell of a lot that can go wrong, and there are other calls to make. Three more companies- three of the biggest investors in Green City. One or two of whom Anthony would have called friends before Chambers had turned them against him and NexCorp.

It isn't healthy to think of them as friends, not after what they have done to him. It's time to pay them back. It's time to show them what happens when they pick the wrong side of history.

"This meeting has to be perfect, Moira," he says. "I want it to play out exactly like you imagined."

Moira just smiles at pressure like that, as she always does. "Come with me, sir. Let me show you what I'm setting up."

***

Moira leads him up the stairs to the very top floor of the NexCorp building. It's a room that Anthony doesn't use much- only for interviews and meetings with potential investors. It's a room that provides panoramic views of Green City. Just with a quick glance out the window, he can see the main centers of operation for the other companies that he now considers his rivals.

Chambers's own building is just a few blocks away- a towering skyscraper with tinted windows adorned with the huge corporate font of the company name Chambers Energy.

Moira has set the room up exactly as Anthony had imagined. He will be sat on one side, and the four of them- Chambers and his turncoat allies- will be sat opposite. Forced to sit alongside each other like the team they claim to be. Bruce is there as well, ensuring that the terms of the proposed deal are laid out clearly and placed on a projector screen that everyone will be able to see.

"I've fully encrypted everything," he says. "If Denise still has some desire to snoop through her files, there's no way she will be able to get into this. The deal exists only on NexCorp's servers. It will delete itself as soon as Chambers and the others leave the boardroom. It will be like it never existed at all."

"You're sure he won't suspect anything?" Anthony asks him.

"I wouldn't say it if I wasn't, boss. We've got all the cards this time."

"You look like shit Bruce. Have you been sleeping?"

Bruce manages a grin, even with his black-ringed, bloodshot eyes. "Finished at midnight last night," he says. "I was in here at five this morning. I tried to sleep. I kept on thinking of new risks involved with bringing them into the office and then planned ways to avoid them. Can't be helped."

Anthony knew that Bruce wasn't one to accept praise. That he would downplay whatever Anthony said and he would keep his stony, grouchy exterior intact. Rather than say anything, Anthony just put a hand on his shoulder. One firm squeezes to let a man know how appreciated he is.

My team is everything to me, Anthony thinks. This is what loyalty looks like. He promises himself that he will never take them for granted ever again.

***

The next day, the office holds its breath. To any stranger wandering into NexCorp, it might look as though Anthony simply runs a very tight ship there at the company. People are silent, heads down, quietly clacking away on keyboards and quietly discussing ideas. Blinds are drawn in every office. Meetings are underway in quiet rooms. It seems as though every desk is filled- as though no one is taking a day off.

Anthony knows the difference. Every person there, by now, is aware of the stakes of the meeting that evening. He can guess what's going through their heads. They are wondering what news they are going to get tomorrow. They will be wondering if they have to start looking for jobs. Anthony is sure that many of them will have started to look for new jobs already, protecting themselves from any potential outcome.

The biggest difference is the looks he gets from those that he passes. Ordinarily, a stroll through the office, for Anthony, means conversations starting in every room. It means people are looking to clap him on the back or ask him what he's getting up to that weekend.

Now, there is none of that. People just give him a firm nod- almost a confirmation that they are feeling what he's feeling.

"Keep going," Anthony says to everyone when he meets their eye. "I know it's daunting. Just keep working. I'm going to do everything I can to make this word."

He cancels any other meetings that day. He skips lunch entirely. He finds himself running through the facts and figures that Moira collected for him a dozen times, practicing in his head as he looks at them, imagining exactly what he's going to say and how he's going to say it. Every word needs to have an impact. The difference between these businessmen needs to come to light.

He keeps on ruminating and planning until the hours slip away and it's dark outside. Moira knocks on his door to wish him good luck, as well as Bruce, Harvey, and a dozen other faces from the office.

"I'll let you all know how it goes," he tells them. "As soon as I can."

***

Anthony waits down in reception by himself. He's sent Annie home, intending to greet Chambers personally at the others. He knows, to them, that will probably look a little strange, as though he's doing his own grunt work. But Anthony doesn't care- he wants to be fully in control of the situation from the moment they walk through the door.

They do not arrive all at once. The first to arrive is Kelly Walker- CEO and Director of Walker Solutions. She doesn't look anything like any other CEO that Anthony has ever met. She's wearing bright-rimmed glasses and her grey hair tied down in dreadlocks. The first thing she does as she enters is offer Anthony a big hug, which Anthony rejects, opting instead for a handshake. "Different times," he says, by way of explanation. "Last time you were here, we were allies through and through."

"We can be allies again, Tony. I suppose we just need a different strategy. Shall we go up to your office?"

Anthony shakes his head. "We've got a few others arriving."

Walker frowns at that but takes a seat at one of the stools around the reception area. She looks as out of place in Anthony's modern corporate office as Anthony would at a farmer's market.

The next to arrive is Rick Yewtree. He walks through the office front door and looks at Walker as though she's some sort of alien. "I thought this was a closed meeting," he says. "We are supposed to be talking business."

"We will," says Anthony. "I don't believe I ever promised you an exclusive use of my time, Mr. Yewtree. I need to speak to each of you."

Yewtree sighs. "I suppose this isn't going to be a quick one then, is it?"

Anthony does not confirm nor deny. He leaves Yewtree to sit down and place his briefcase on top of a table, which he drums his fingers on top of, echoing impatiently.

When Helda Zenata arrives, it begins to become quite clear to each of them that this meeting isn't quite what they had expected. "This better not be a stunt, Tony," she says. "I know you're sore about what happened with Chambers. We never wanted to work with that asshole, but you didn't give us much choice."

"That asshole has just pulled up," says Anthony.

All three of the "Big Three" go a little pale. They at once look outside at the familiar Rolls Royce that has just pulled up. Chambers enters reception wearing a smug grin. A grin starts to appear when he sees the "Big Three" sitting around there. He stands in the entranceway with a frown, neither stepping into the building nor walking away from it. He's got an expression on his face like he's forgotten something. Anthony suppresses the urge to smile. For once, Chambers isn't grinning. He hadn't been expecting this.

"Ladies and gentlemen," says Anthony. "Shall we go up to the boardroom?"

***

It's cold in the boardroom. Cold enough that people look uncomfortable in their seats, shaking slightly and avoiding putting their bare arms on the tables and chairs. The heating is on a timer- it goes off after office hours. Anthony's used to it. He stays late often and doesn't so much as quake. He's glad the other four of them look uncomfortable, though. he needs to do anything that he can to increase the tension between them.

They pull their chairs away from each other, spreading as far apart as they can on the other side of the boardroom table. Chambers himself is in the middle, directly across from Anthony. They don't speak between them. It occurs to Anthony that, most likely, the four of them had never been in the same room together. Most likely, whatever deal the Chambers arranged between them, it was one that was handled by their cronies.

"The deal I want to propose affects all of you. That's why I've called you here today," says Anthony.

"I don't see how it could," says Chambers. "We are not working together, Little Tony. My rivals and fellow business leaders here simply made sense of the flaws in your scheme and app when I explained them to them. You must be quite paranoid if you think we've created a little conspiracy against you."

"Paranoia has very little to do with it, Mr. Chambers. I don't really care why all three of you removed your investment- though I suspect Mr. Chambers's lawyers and his often threatening demeanor may have had something to do with it. All I care about is that I revitalize some of the money I lost. I believe we can find a way forward in which LevelUp is not a threat to any of you."

"You better be careful with what you're saying, boy."

"Please relax, Robert. I think we can all be honest here without any need to beat around the bush."

Chambers doesn't relax. His face has gone a shade of puce. No people skills- the man had never been good at direct confrontation. He barely ever played his hand until he was sure he was holding aces. He hadn't been expected to sit with his allies today, and he feels as though he is out of control.

Don't push it, though, Anthony reminds himself. He doesn't want to annoy Chambers enough that the man just gets up and walks out of the room. He needs him there. He needs to fracture their alliance.

He turns on the project in the room, showing the same presentation that Moira used in the boardroom just a couple of days before. It lays out each company represented in that room, as well as their expansion plans covering the next few years.

"Walker, you're planning to revolutionize the local power grid," he says. "Very admirable. We promise LevelUp won't get in the way of that. We'll keep our green power investments outside of the local area. Chambers, at the same time, you want to expand your coal plant. Fine, we'll stay out of your way as well. Phillip Sterling, we'll leave you to your own private investments. And Z, we won't interfere in any of your new plans to build super-computers and high-energy servers in the city." He smiles. "All of your plans will remain intact because LevelUp is no longer going to operate in Green City. In fact, if you agree, we'll completely change our corporate headquarters. We will set up again in a city that has no affiliation at all with any of your business practices so that you can all work on your expansions in peace."

"I can't believe you want to expand a coal power plant," says Walker, locking vicious eyes at Chambers. "You know that will be a failure, right? The mayor agreed to a green energy supply."

"Mayor's change, Walker. Let's not get distracted. Besides-" he turns his attention on Yewtree- "politics will be the least of our worries. You're investing an awful lot in our competitor, Yewtree. You know you can't change the dominant energy providers in Green City. I simply won't allow it."

"What you will and won't allow is quite a boring topic, Chambers," says Yewtree.

"None of you will provide enough power to make my servers into a reality," says Zenata. "And you should all give up. AI is the fastest-growing industry in the United States. Whatever power we need, we'll get. And we don't intend to have your help in securing contracts."

Their voices are starting to rise. There is a bitter edge to everything that they're saying. Anthony sits back, careful not to interrupt. He lets them trade barbs back and forth as he fondles the drive in his pocket.

The bread crumbs that Denise gave him are there. He also adds the story he received from Gloria about Chambers's private theft from companies he has been a part of. As well as a few other choice bits. It's his final weapon- his nuclear bomb. He needs to wait for the right time to unleash it.

"That's enough talking," grunts Chambers. He does so loud enough to shut up the room. "It doesn't matter anyway, does it? You all agree with me about letting LevelUp die so we forget our differences."

"You promised you would stand aside and not get in the way of our projects," said Walker.

"We will discuss that afterward. In private- not in a boardroom controlled by the very man who wants to destroy us." Chambers put a trademark grin on his face, though for once, it seemed a little forced. "It's very clever of you, Tony- trying to turn us against each other. But we're not squabbling children. We've made an agreement between each of us that we do not want to see LevelUp succeed. If this deal is the best you can propose, then we will need time to consider if we can accept it. You'll give us ten minutes to discuss?"

"With pleasure," says Anthony, standing. He leaves the room but makes sure to keep the presentation open on the projector on the wall. It shows the slide explaining the differences between the four big companies in black-and-white terms.

He goes out into the hallway and watches the conversation taking place inside. It becomes increasingly more animated as time goes by. Chambers is turning left and right, being berated on all sides by his different allies.

They don't *look* like a room full of united allies. Perhaps Moira's plan can really work. He continues to fiddle with the flash drive in his pocket. He doesn't want to use it- not if he can avoid it. Nothing about Chambers's corruption has ever been proven, and he knows that making any accusation will lead to a swift and heavy retribution by Chambers.

Eventually, the room goes quiet. No one inside looks happy, but Chambers stands up and opens the door, glaring at Anthony as he does so. "We're ready to discuss your deal," he says.

Chapter 9:

Redemption or Greed

"We're not happy to agree," says Chambers. "Not until you can provide some sort of assurances that you won't later side with one of us over the others."

"I've already said that I don't intend to get involved with any of the businesses in this room."

"That isn't what we're talking about."

"Ah. You don't trust each other, is that it? If you think one of you will come back to LevelUp, we will help support them in getting dominance in Green City. Rest assured, that isn't how we do things here. We are not focused on profit, and we do not help larger businesses assert dominance. We believe all companies- large or small deserve a fair chance to compete in the international market." He sighs. "Really, after all this time, and none of you *really* understand what NexCorp is trying to achieve, do you?"

Chambers shakes his head. "Come off it, Anthony. I know you talk a good game, but business is business. We all say things that we need to say in order to get ahead."

"Some of you more so than others."

Chambers grins. "I take that as a compliment, Little Tony," he says. "There's a reason you've lost here today. There's a reason your NexCorp is breathing its last few breaths. Business and ruthlessness are the same thing. Profits only happen when you can get them in a stranglehold and never let them go. You either get rich, or you try and help everyone. You can't do both. It's better to help the people who matter. Like my associates in this room."

Anthony carefully studies the faces of the "Big Three" as Chambers talks. They scowl at him as though they don't agree with a word he's saying. Moira was right- this alliance really is paper thin.

Time to put the final nail in the coffin.

"Actually, Robert, I think you may have misidentified the priorities of your friends here," says Anthony. "I've been carrying out an awful lot of research into all of you. Doubtless, Chambers Energy's own business practices are quite unique. You're an old-world titan, aren't you, Mr. Chambers? With some old school business practices."

"Another compliment, as far as I'm concerned."

"If you say so."

Anthony plugs the flash drive in his pocket into the projector. At once, the old presentation vanishes. It is replaced by a scan of the financial records that Gloria had shown him. It includes the scans of the money embezzled from his father's company.

Walker, Zenata, and Sterling all squint- they've no idea what they're looking at. But Chambers's face goes quite pale. "What is this?" he says. "Those look like private documents!"

"They were given to me in trust. In case your colleagues are confused here, these are the details of an offshore bank account that Chambers held a long time ago. Inside, there are the profits he made from his very first venture- all un-taxed and mostly stolen. Untraceable, until now."

Chambers's eyes are like cold steel. There is hate there and vengeance. Anthony knows he's crossed a line from which there's no coming back. But his future- his vision for the future- hangs in the balance.

"Before we move on with any deal," he continues. "I just want to make sure that my old friends- my "Big Three" investors- remember who they are choosing to side with. When I first talked to all of you about LevelUp, it was because I wanted to make business a force for good again. And you all used to agree with me on that. I just want to ask you- colleagues- what changed? Did he threaten you? Did he bribe you?"

An exchange of glances. Anthony must be on the mark.

"This is ludicrous slander," says Chambers. "You understand I was giving you kindness by taking your investors away? I could destroy you. I could have destroyed you at any point during your little experiment."

Anthony ignores him. He is speaking only to the "Big Three"- taking the time to lock eyes with Zenata, Walker, and Sterling in turn. "You see how long this man has been doing this for? Do you think he's going to stop? The history of Chambers Energy is filled with constant betrayals, back-stabs, and shady deals. You can turn against NexCorp now, but rest assured that Chambers will turn against you in the future. Or you can break the cycle. You can be part of a system that actually has the chance to knock men like Chambers from their oversized pedestals.

"So, actually, my good friends, I'm here to offer you two deals today. You can take the first deal I've already described to you, which involves me leaving Green City and you continuing to work with Chambers. Or you can take the second deal. Your investment in LevelUp once again, with the same terms as before. No hard feelings- and an open platform for us to work together, with honest communication."

"This is ridiculous," says Chambers. "None of this changes anything. The man is still utterly mad! He wants to tear down our businesses, can't you see that?"

"We'd like to have another discussion, I think," says Sterling coolly.

"Very well. A good idea- I'm sure we can get all of this straightened out."

"Without you in the room, please, Mr. Chambers."

Chambers's eyes look fat, bulging, and bloodshot, like they're about to jump out of his skull in his fury and dance across the table.

But his three "allies" are all shooting him sharp, expectant looks.

He walks out of the room. Anthony follows him. Leaving the "Big Three" to discuss both of their fates.

***

"You can't smoke in here," says Anthony.

"Bite me," says Chambers, as he lights up a cigar.

Anthony doesn't argue any further. He just opens a window. After all, the smoke alarms are not in the area directly outside the boardroom. If Chambers needs to smoke in order to have a tantrum, he guesses, he might as well let him do it.

Inside the boardroom, the Big Three investors are engaged in an incredibly lively debate. They are standing, sitting, raising voices, and lowering them again. Twenty minutes have passed already. Anthony is watching them with a steady gaze.

He feels a complete sense of calm. This is it, after all. Every single one of his cards has been laid on the table. Every bit of ammunition that he has against Chambers has been fired. His future, now, is in the hands of those investors. They are the people who can either set a course toward a bright business future, or they can strangle those hopes before they have a chance to bloom.

The room fills with the unpleasant, throat-tickling dryness of secondhand smoke. Chambers coughs every time he breathes in. To Anthony, Chambers looks even older than his 45 years. His face is veined and sagging, and his smell is stale and smoky. For the first time in Anthony's eyes, the man looks tired. It's like he has been wearing a mask the whole time- the mask of a dynamic, ruthless, energetic businessman. Now, he is just wearing the worried mask of an old man, afraid that his life's work is about to be taken away from him.

"Where in the hell did you find those documents, Little Tony?" he hisses. "Even I didn't know those existed. Did you fake them?"

"I don't tend to fake things, Robert. I've always found that lying can get you in hot water if you do it too often." He gestures to the boardroom. "I guess this is evidence of that."

"You know this won't change anything. Your app is doomed to fail, no matter how many investors you get."

"I know that's what you think."

"I've got ten years more experience than you in this game, kid. And I learned from my father. It doesn't matter what good intentions people have when they start a business; it's the ruthless that survive. Those people who are willing to clamber over the others to the top get to have success. It isn't pretty, but that's how it goes." He exhales a lungful of smoke as though to punctuate his sentence. "It's a dog-eat-dog world, kid. And only the meanest, biggest dogs survive."

Anthony takes in what Chambers saying with more attention than the man would usually deserve. There is a difference in Chambers's voice now- a certainty, one that has been deadset by age and experience. For once, Anthony guesses that Chambers is saying what he actually thinks, which has to be a pretty rare occurrence by Anthony's reckoning.

"Does it really feel good?" Anthony says. "Having more money than most people could dream of? Does it really feel right that you get to go and eat at the Ritz every night when people in this city have to go to food banks? Have to live in the dark and cold because they can't afford their bills?"

Chambers shrugs. "Any one of them could do what you or I can do."

"Of course they can't. You and I are both from rich families, Robert. Our parents gave us opportunities. They encouraged us. We learned from them what went right in business and what went wrong, and then when they died, we got huge fat inheritances from them. You and I have money because we took risks on business ideas. Because we could afford to take those risks- because those risks weren't really risks. If our money ran out, we knew we had more waiting for us, tied up with our families. Ordinary people don't get that chance. LevelUp gives them that chance, do you see? They can push the risk on to people who can afford it."

"People should look after themselves. Help is a two-way street."

"Sure is," says Anthony. "You never helped anyone, did you, Robert? And now you're about to see what happens from a life lived selfishly."

"You can't possibly think that they are going to side with you."

"I think there are more good people out there than you think, Chambers. And good people together can do way, way more than a selfish person who casts himself apart." Anthony nods his head towards the boardroom door. "Let's find out if the Big Three are good people, shall we?"

The Big Three have stopped talking. Walker is making eye contact with Anthony, beckoning him forward. Anthony smiles at Chambers, who looks as though he is about to be sick. He looks weaker than Anthony has ever seen him. Perhaps some of what he had just said had managed to make its way into the man's thick skull at last?

***

"We've considered both deals," says Sterling. "And we would like to propose a deal of our own."

Anthony and Chambers exchange a glance. They are both sat on the same side of the table, and it feels bizarre to be being pitched to at the same time as his rival.

"We wish to become a part of LevelUp," Walker adds. "On the same terms as before. After discussing it, we truly do believe that this platform can be the future of business. It might just be the vehicle that helps us to cut through petty squabbles and truly help society."

Anthony sits up, smiling, ready to shake hands. But the Big Three are still quiet on the other side of the board room, their faces stoic. Zenata is next to talk.

"Having said that," she says. "We do not believe this platform can work in Green City whilst a corrupt and powerful man like Chambers keeps trying to dismantle it. He will continue to put other investors against us, and he will be able to build alliances that crush any new businesses before they have a chance to grow and prosper.

"We, therefore, put it to you that we can only move ahead if Chambers agrees to set aside a huge portion of his own wealth in support of LevelUp. He needs to be involved as well so we can ensure a united front for the businesses of Green City."

Silence. Anthony's mouth falls open on a rare occasion of speechlessness. It was a ridiculous proposal. A caveat that was never going to work. Chambers had created *conferences* specifically to target NexCorp. He'd created rival apps. He'd threatened and intimidated politicians to speak against the platform!

"There has to be some wiggle room there," says Anthony. "We all know that you are asking for the impossible. We can do a great job without Chambers. Together, we can bring him down!"

"With all due respect, Anthony," says Walker. "I've known you for many years now, and I've been in business a lot longer. You're a dreamer, Tony, and a brilliant one. But you have next to no sense when it comes to the realities of running a business. An enemy like Chambers is too much for your app to take on. It's big, but it's not big enough yet. And it will never get big and popular with someone like Chambers manipulating you at every turn."

"You supported us before."

"Yes. Before, you showed us evidence of Chambers's willingness to stamp out his competition. And before Chambers began threatening and bribing us himself. Business is business, Tony, as much as we'd all like it to be something else." She turns back to Chambers. "You need to accept Robert, or this whole thing is dead in the water."

"He's not going to accept."

"Thank you, Tony. I'm speaking to Mr. Chambers now."

Anthony sighs. He turns to Chambers with a sinking feeling in his stomach, knowing that he's already lost. There's no way in the world that a man like Chambers is going to agree with the terms and conditions of LevelUp.

But Chambers doesn't dismiss the question straight away. He still looks pale, old, and tired. He takes a long drag on his cigar before finally answering.

"Explain to me how this app works again," he says. "Explain to me how it's going to help me and how it's going to help other people."

Anthony stares at him, scanning for sarcasm, but Chambers's question seems genuine. Walker laughs.

"You're in for quite a treat, Robert. Mr. Brown's pitches are like nothing else I've ever seen. On your feet, Mr. Brown- one last time for your old rival."

***

Anthony goes from the very start. He explains how the idea came to him- how he has always seen the world in the same way, as a linked series of organizations, all supporting each other. He explains how selfish organizations became broken cogs that ruined the whole machine. They sit and grow and grow, extracting energy from the other cogs in the system whilst refusing to turn.

Big, powerful companies rule the world, he explains. They get so much money that it's almost impossible to knock them down from their positions of authority, even when their business ideas are fundamentally flawed and outdated and not what the world needs. They get so big and powerful that no one can convince them that new ideas are better. The old ideas were what helped them to become giants, so they stuck to those old ideas and crushed anything that might threaten them.

He explains that big companies have to take ownership of their unique position. Instead of seeing themselves as the naturally dominant forces in any market, they have to accept that they hold the most power. Their influence can make or break new, potentially better- ideas from spawning and being allowed to grow.

"Hence the need for LevelUp," says Anthony, at last. "Everyone wins. Money from big companies gets moved around, and they get to have investment opportunities in the businesses of the future. You could get your foot on the ladder in a green energy firm, supporting them with your success whilst also future-proofing your own supply. You could even venture out into a business you've never even considered before, making profits in a whole new area. Ultimately, you can only buy a maximum of 5% of any new business. They will ultimately be in charge of their idea. But that 5% could turn into something incredibly valuable if you were to succeed in creating the next big idea that changes the world."

"But I'm the one with the money," says Chambers. "If I'm putting money into these businesses, I should own them. 51% at minimum. It shouldn't be a difficult deal- it's either get my investment or fail."

"Or they go with another company on the platform that is offering the same amount at a lower percentage. They get rich, and you don't get any of it because you insisted on being bullheaded about everything." Anthony shrugs. "The platform is a new way of looking at things, Robert. You have to either work with the rules or don't be a part of it. It's as simple as that. But I urge you to think not just about the money you can make but about the people you could help in the future as well. For most people, starting a business is a pipe dream. You could make those dreams into realities."

"Either way," Walker adds. "Your public image is going to need some help after all of this. We're sick of keeping quiet about your corruption, Chambers. If you don't side with us on this, we're going to become a hell of a lot more vocal about what we know."

Chambers sneers at her. "So you're threatening me, as well? What a truly fair proposal this is."

"With all due respect, Robert, we're only repaying you in kind for how each of you has been treated in the past."

Chambers opens his mouth to argue and then closes it again. Anthony can't quite believe it. Never, in all his life, did he ever think that he would see Chambers's speechless. But it seems the man has run out of arguments. He's put himself into a corner- a victim of his own arrogance and his belief in his ability to extort and cajole against opposition.

Looking around at the untied front of the "Big Three" is almost enough to make Anthony cry. He had always told people that he believed business could be good. He had to admit, over the course of the last few weeks since the launch of LevelUp, that his firmness in that belief was beginning to shake.

But here was the proof- allies sat across from each other in a boardroom, working together on a deal for the benefit of society rather than themselves. *This is what the future is going to look like*, Anthony tells himself. He wondered whether he was witnessing the very first sign of a cultural shift. A new face for business worldwide, matching his dreams and his visions.

"Fine," says Chambers, eventually. "It'll fail- mark my words-it'll fail. But it seems, for the moment, that it's far more effort to be against you than with you, Little Tony."

"You're serious?" Anthony says.

Chambers shrugs. "You'll have my money. Some of it, anyway. And you better believe that I will be *scrutinizing* the business plans of your users before I even think of handing them my hard-earned funds." He grins. "I'll admit you give a good pitch, Little Tony. I think your father would be quite proud."

"I think he would be as resistant and arrogant about my ideas as you are, Robert. But I still appreciate the gesture." He smiles, turning on the charm that he's had to put in his back pocket for too long now, tense as he's been about the negotiations and the launch of LevelUp. "It's a deal then! I always know you'd come through. Shall we have a drink? Walker- I didn't get a chance to share a champagne with you at the launch partner. Come on. To success!"

Chapter 10:

The New Era

The next week proves to be the fastest moving and wildest of Anthony's life. The very next day, he posted on the company website that all four of Green City's "Big Four" were now signed on to LevelUp. Barely three minutes after he posts it, his phone starts ringing. People and interviewers from all across the country want to speak to him, calling the new union of the four companies "extraordinary."

"I guess that they can't believe that someone like Chambers would be on LevelUp," Moria says when Anthony gets off the phone. "I can't quite believe it either."

"I don't like it," says Bruce.

"You don't like anything," says Anthony.

"True though that is, I have to agree with Bruce on this one," says Moira. "This man was trying to destroy us completely just a few days ago. Maybe he's got his own reasons for coming into the business. Maybe he's just biding his time. Plus, he still hasn't closed down that ridiculous app he's using to try and compete with us."

"You weren't there in the interview room, guys. This is different this time. He looked like the wind had been finally knocked out of his sails." He leans forward over his desk and pours a glass of the champagne he brought since no one else seems to want to pour any. "Remember, today is about celebrating, you two. I need to thank you for everything you've done. Your efforts have stopped NexCorp from going bankrupt. Now, we can start planning for the future."

Moira takes the glass that Anthony offers her with just a half smile. "I suppose it just seems too good to be true," she says. "But perhaps this time, I'll go along with your enthusiasm. It's just too hard to say no to you when you're like this, sir. Like telling off a happy dog."

She sips and raises a glass. Anthony meets hers with his own.

Bruce, across from them, keeps his arms folded. "I'm sure as hell not celebrating," he says. "Not when you've introduced just about the biggest security risk I can imagine. You've given Chambers access to the system, Anthony. He's going to study it and its flaws. You've given him a way to plan how to bring us down."

"You think he wouldn't have found that out for himself at some point, Bruce?" says Anthony. "Look, a few days ago, we were getting ready to end forever. Now, we get to survive for a little while longer. Surely that- no matter what- is worth celebrating!"

He holds out a glass for Bruce to take. Bruce looks at it with a stern face, then he sighs, takes the glass, and takes a sip. "Fine," he says. "You really are like a puppy dog, Anthony. What's the matter with you?"

"I can see change, guys," he says. "Things I've been dreaming about for a long time, finally unfolding. It's more exciting now than ever. Our start-up problems have been conquered."

"Does that mean you're going to work shorter hours?"

"Well. I finished at five today. I have to stay in till nine tomorrow, though, to start on strategies moving forward."

"Naturally," says Moira with a grin. "Well, considering this is the closest you ever get to taking time off, Tony, let's go and celebrate for real. We'll go to that new cocktail bar across the street. My treat."

***

The Big Four Become the Big Five

NexCorp- Who Will They Bag Next?

Anthony reads the headlines over and over. They aren't just on local papers, either. It seems his face- as well as the faces of his latest investors- are on just about every single news outlet that he looks at. It's a dizzying experience, but at least he doesn't have to worry about getting berated on the street anymore. The only thing he has to worry about now is people stopping to take selfies with him, which he's getting used to, even if he does think it's a bit of a waste of time. He didn't get into business as part of a popularity contest after all. He wants to tell them to go and start working on their own ideas instead of chasing famous people around.

On Monday, he goes out on his own for the first time since he was nearly attacked in the main plaza. Just as he's about to leave the front door, Bruces comes up to him.

"You really want to go out there on your own?" he says. "I know things are a bit better, but you're still better off being safe than sorry."

"Got to go out at some point, Bruce."

"You've got your phone on you?"

"Course boss." Anthony taps his pocket sarcastically, grinning as he does so. Bruce does not look amused. "Look, Bruce, I've got to start taking risks some time. Besides, I've got a couple of places that I've got to go visit."

"Just get an Uber. And stay out of trouble!"

***

Anthony's first stop isn't somewhere he expected to be visiting again. Not when the last time he had been there was so painful.

In the daytime, Denise's apartment looks sadder than it does at night. He can see the graffiti on the walls, and there is a slight smog in the air from the nearby highway. He knows he paid Denise a fair wage, but the woman had never had the guts to go out and get something better for herself. In her mind, this sort of place was what she deserved. It was what she had always known.

Anthony takes the lift this time, and he does so calmly, without the need to rush. He goes to Denise's front door and doesn't intend to knock, just to slide the letter underneath the gap between the door and the floor. But, as soon as he does that, it swings open anyway.

Denise is standing there with a cigarette in her hand. To Anthony's knowledge, she hasn't smoked since university. When she sees Anthony, her eyes widen for just a second before going cold and hard.

"Guess you won, Tony," she says. "Here to gloat?"

"Have you ever known me to gloat?"

"Of course not. But I've never known you to have such a big win before." She runs a hand through her hair. "He's not come back, you know- not since the day you caught him here. He can be charming Tony. A good liar."

A good liar. He had sounded so sincere when he had agreed to a deal in the boardroom. Was it possible he was lying then as well?

"I'm not here for any reason other than to say sorry. I don't feel right about what happened before you left. I was swept up in everything, and I didn't give you the appreciation you deserve. I can't forgive you for what you've done in response. Not yet, anyway. But just know that I'm sorry."

Denise frowns. "That's it?" she says. "No business to discuss? No deals to make?"

Anthony smiles. "It's a personal call."

"Never thought I'd hear those words coming out of your mouth, Tony."

"Me neither."

"Will you come in for coffee?"

Anthony shakes his head. "I've got lots to get on with."

"It won't take long."

"We can't be friends again. Not after everything."

Denise nods. Her eyes have gone all glassy like she might cry. Anthony leaves before she does. In truth, he's feeling a little emotional as well, seeing her again. But he had to have closure. Denise might have tried to ruin his life, but there had been many years before that when they had spent hours and hours in the same room together. It was hard to let something like that go, especially when he hadn't been the perfect boss for her in the past.

He jumps back into his Uber. There's one more stop that he needs to get to.

***

It's a different experience this time, getting out in the suburban streets of outer Green City. There are still members of the public who look as though they could hurt people, who look at the lowest ebbs of their life, but seeing Anthony, they break into smiles. A man in a black hoodie with a gold tooth even stops to take a selfie with him, all grins.

"I see it now," the stranger says. "You're gonna fix this place, ain't you? I know it, man. I can see it in your eyes. Hey, I got a business idea, you know. Might need to change a few laws to make it work, though."

Anthony slips away as quickly and politely as he can, then knocks on Gloria's door.

"Who the hell is it?" rasps her voice from the other side of the wood.

"Is that any way to speak to family, Aunt Gloria?"

Gloria opens the door, her face as impassive and unimpressed as ever. He waves Anthony in with a grumble and, this time goes straight to making him a coffee. He sits down on her sofa, feeling a little more comfortable than he had the first time he had been around. When Gloria brings him his coffee, she even pats him on the shoulder- the most sincere gesture of affection that Anthony had seen yet from the woman.

"Guess you gave my son a change of heart then. I saw on the news he's investing with you. Not that I understand any of that. That letter helped, did it?"

"More than you could possibly know. I couldn't have done this without you, Gloria."

"You blackmail him?"

Anthony grins. "Not my style."

"I'd have blackmailed him. Ungrateful waste of space that he was. What do you want then, more documents?"

"I'm just here to see my Auntie."

"Well, you've seen me. Now pipe down, I'm watching *Grey's Anatomy*."

She doesn't even mention the bouquet of flowers that Anthony was holding. He sets them down on the table in front of him and stays sitting through as much TV as he can bear. He isn't one for sitting still in front of a screen for any long period of time. The last time he watched TV properly had been when he was a kid.

When he gets up to leave, he gives a hearty goodbye. Gloria grunts, as she often does, but just as he's about to leave the house, she shouts. "Thanks. For the flowers. No one bought flowers since the 90s. Good luck, kid. Come round any time."

"I will, Auntie Gloria."

The woman chuckles. It's a heartwarming sound to hear coming from the crotchety old woman's mouth. Anthony can't help but smile as he leaves and goes back onto the street to wait for his cab.

He wonders how she'll react the moment she finds the check wrapped up in the bouquet. Anthony doesn't want it to look like charity. It was just what he deemed she deserved to be paid for the hold she's given and the hard life she's had. Probably enough to get some repairs done on the house, at least. Maybe enough for a vacation as well.

He hadn't had family for a long time. This time, he was going to keep the bridges strong for as long as he could.

****

Anthony notices that his Uber is taking a strange route back to the office. Rather than cutting straight into the business district, the driver takes them along the coast road that runs just across from the main beach, with all of its resorts and hotels. Naturally, the traffic is jammed up. It was only supposed to be a twenty-minute drive. Now they're further away from the office than when they started, and it's been half an hour.

Also, the driver is looking at Anthony in the rearview mirror every few seconds or so, like he knows he's gone wrong but doesn't want to say anything.

"Did I give you the wrong address?" Anthony asks him.

"No. Sorry, sir, this is unusual. But a friend of yours called me. They say they want me to take you to the Generation Hotel."

"A friend? Who?"

"A woman. Her name was Moira."

"Right. Okay." He pulls out his phone. There's one text from her- it just says, "See you soon!"

He's already feeling as though he's wasted time leaving the office for so long. Now Moira is pulling him away even longer! Well, he had no idea what this was about. But if Moira has planned it, then it must be important. The woman was not a time-waster either.

****

Arriving at the Generation Hotel, Anthony gets a huge rush of deja vu. The car park is filled to bursting again. Here and there are dotted staff members and investors, sharing cigarettes and sipping drinks, who all cheer as he steps out of the car. Among them is Bruce, who, for once, has a grin stretching from ear to ear.

"Glad you could make it, Tony," he says. "Moira was worried you'd cancel on us. Too busy, or some guff like that."

"What the hell is this?"

"You're celebration party."

"And one that was supposed to be a surprise," says Moira, now appearing from the main entrance to the building. "You need to slow down on the whiskey, Bruce."

Bruce waves away the comment before sparking up another cigarette. He does look a little drunk, but then so does everyone. The smiles, grins, and laughter they're all sharing are infectious.

"What are we celebrating?" Anthony said. "Getting the "Big Three"- or "Big Four" now, I guess- back? I wish you had said, Moira. I know it's nice, but the budget isn't going to last if we have a party every single time and something goes well."

She giggles. "I *know* you wouldn't have read the news. We aren't paying for a penny of this; we're being sponsored by our advertisers."

"Advertisers? I didn't know they had this kind of money."

"They do now."

She holds up a phone for Anthony to see. It's the front page of the Green City Gazette. The main headline is there- *Is Green City the New Silicone Valley? LevelUp Breaks Records for Most Downloaded App of All Time.*

Anthony feels his jaw-dropping. He knew that they would start doing well now that they had their investors back on board, but *all the time?* The article said that they had almost two billion downloads. Business ideas from Europe, China, and Africa were loaded onto the platform.

Plus, there are record numbers of new investors joining every day without Anthony even needing to arrange meetings with them.

The list of company names of people involved is staggering. Anthony sees several from the *Forbes 500* list.

"You said you were going to build a new world, Anthony," says Moira. "Welcome to your new world! Now, come on, you need to give a speech. The world press is waiting."

Feeling as though he is in a dream, Anthony follows Moira into the function room. She's not lying- amongst the party-goers are several photographers, all of whom animate into action as soon as Anthony steps into the room. He is almost dazed by the flashing of bulbs on their camera and overwhelmed by the cheer and applause that greets him.

"Thank you, everyone," he says, adapting quickly, as he usually does. "You can't know how good it feels to watch your dreams turning into reality before your eyes, and I hope all of our new users feel that the platform helps them to realize their own dreams as well. Every single staff member at NexCorp has contributed towards making this a reality, and I want to thank every single one of them for more than making up for my faults when it comes to running a business."

More applause. Then, one of the reporters present in the room raises a hand. Anthony is surprised for just a moment- he isn't used to taking questions like this from people outside of the office. "Go on," he says.

"I want to know what's next, sir," the reporter says. "You say you want to change the world. How does having all of these users help that to happen?"

"Because now the money can move. This is just the start of everyone's hard work. We've got investors. We've got the ideas from the people. Connecting the two will be the start of a new world- a world where everyone gets access to the financial resources they need. We're fighting for economic equality- that's the long and short of it. Starting tomorrow, we're going to make sure that our investors' money is going to start moving towards the people who need it most.

There is an applause then louder than Anthony has ever heard before, at any point in his life. He is passed from person to person, reporter to reporter. He catches the eye of his Big Four but doesn't have enough time to do anything but smile and grin. Even the chamber is there. Does the man look happy? Anthony isn't sure. But he's keeping himself to himself, which is the next best thing.

***

Anthony doesn't get a moment of peace until he's back in his office. He hasn't drunk, so he feels ready to get back to work. It's late, and there's no one else there. They're all still either partying or they've gone home, and Anthony knows it's going to be a slow day at the office tomorrow. He doesn't mind- this celebration is warranted, and his team has worked immensely hard to get him out of this crisis.

He turns on his computer. There are thousands of emails in his inbox, some marked with names he's never heard of, inviting him to events all over the globe. Just at a glance, he sees a dozen potential opportunities- ways for even more money to be active on LevelUp's servers, which are ready for users to access.

He takes a deep breath and starts typing. Starting tomorrow, it's going to be the dawn of his new world. He intends to be out there, making the most of every chance he can get, to improve people's lives.

www.ingramcontent.com/pod-product-compliance
Lightning Source LLC
Chambersburg PA
CBHW071445130726
47997CB00006B/2235